My House, Your City

Fernanda Canales

My House, Your City
Privacy in a Shared World

For María, Francisco and Carlos

Original edition: *Mi casa, tu ciudad. Privacidad en un mundo compartido* (2021), updated second edition published by Puente editores, Barcelona, 2024.

First published by
Verlag der Buchhandlung Walther und Franz König
Ehrenstrasse 4
D-50672 Köln, Germany
verlag@buchhandlung-walther-koenig.de

Bibliographical information published by the Deutsche Nationalbibliothek. The Deutsche Nationalbibliothek lists this publication in the Deutsche Nationalbibliographie; detailed bibliographic data are available online at http://dnb.d-nd.de.

Editor: Moisés Puente
Graphic Design: RafamateoStudio
Translation: Jaime Benyei
Proofreading: George Hutton

© of the texts: Fernanda Canales
© of the photographs: their authors
© Verlag der Buchhandlung Walther und Franz König, Cologne, 2024

Printed by GPS in Slovenia
ISBN: 978-3-7533-0697-1

Distribution
Germany, Austria, Switzerland
Buchhandlung Walther König
Ehrenstrasse 4
50672 Cologne, Germany
+49 (0) 221 / 20 59 6 53
verlag@buchhandlung-walther-koenig.de

United States and Canada
D.A.P. / Distributed Art Publishers, Inc.
75 Broad Street, Suite 630
New York, NY 10004, United States
+1 (0) 212 627 1999
orders@dapinc.com

Outside the United States and Canada, Germany, Austria and Switzerland
Thames & Hudson Ltd., London
www.thamesandhudson.com

Contents

7   Foreword
     From Rooms to Communities

11   Introduction
     Moving from Home

19   **Freedom**

23   The House as a Right
29   Free Communities
35   Domestic Revolutions
42   Spatial Freedom

51   **Efficiency**

55   Machines for Living
64   The House as City
69   Shared Lives
74   Houses by Mail
83   Vertical Housing

89   **Wellbeing**

93   A Room of One's Own
99   Personal Paradises for the Future
104   Designed Lives
112   The Ridicule of the Modern House
117   Empire Cabins

129	**Identity**
133	The City in a Building
139	Houses With No Walls
145	Personal Capsules
152	The Inhabitant as a Specialist
163	The Bedroom as a Neighbourhood
175	**Coexistence**
179	The Destruction of the House
191	The Immaterial Dwelling
199	Porous Habitats
210	Between One House and Another
215	Houses that Cooperate
229	**After the House**
231	More than Houses
243	Acknowledgments
245	Image sources

Foreword
From Rooms to Communities

"The house is me or us, whatever we want."

Álvaro Siza

"The house is always the home of others, a space already occupied by other living beings."

Emanuele Coccia

Two hundred years ago, the world was divided in two: the house and the city. The former was for washing clothes, while the latter was for walking around in freshly ironed outfits. The indoor world and the outdoor world. My world and the world of others, night and day. One was for dreaming, and the other was where these dreams could come true. The former for lying down, and the latter for moving around. Two separate spheres, with increasingly divergent trajectories. We've known for a while that this is not true, but today it's unclear in which of these two spheres we produce more or consume more. We know that those who stay at home often have to walk more and carry a heavier burden than those who venture into the hectic life of the city. The French activist Paulette Bernège calculated that the effort required for walking upstairs in a house, five times a day for forty years, was equivalent to carrying the weight of the Eiffel Tower. We now know that there is only one world, and there's no point breaking it into pieces. The 2019 pandemic and the climate crisis have shown that the house is not an isolated realm, detached from the world; this was the intention following the Industrial Revolution, when the division between house and factory caused a rupture between the unproductive and the productive. Today, it cannot really be claimed that people do not work at home, or that life is not dependent on reproductive labour and caregiving. Today, there are no houses for everybody, but the effects of others' houses belong to us all. Houses are a shared entity, even if we shut ourselves away inside them, on our own. The house is not a space, it is not a destination, and it is not an isolated element: houses are ramifications.

The future of the house lies in housing cooperatives and protected social housing; in other words, we need better alternatives for living and having privacy that are not subject to the free market. Houses for living beings, surrounded by living beings, where it is understood that the notion of confinement is mere fiction. Life lies in our interdependencies. We must stop talking about houses, and begin talking about living conditions. How much of yourself do you devote to looking after your house, its costs and everything else related to it? In what way do resources (i.e. water, energy consumption, materials, rubbish) shape our understanding of the house? We cannot keep using the term "emergency housing" when we know that climate and migrant catastrophes are now a daily reality. Rather than waiting for the right moment to rush in and react, why don't we address what's already here?

Just imagine for a moment what would happen if birds outsourced the task of nest-building to those who profit from the shortage of nests. A quick glance at the relationship that any living being (apart from humans, that is) has with its habitat reveals a profound equilibrium between organisms, needs, resources and ecosystems. By contrast, there are clear discrepancies between the houses that we humans want to live in, the houses that suit the planet, and the houses that we actually pay for and clean every day. These discrepancies are due to three falsehoods, the fictitious notions from which the modern house emerged: 1) the house as a place of rest, as if work could be separated from life, and domestic chores would disappear; 2) the house as private property, accessible to all, as if its commodification would not make it, by definition, unaffordable for most; and 3) the house as a sanctuary for the nuclear family (husband, wife and children), as if there were no other forms of coexistence, and as if the private and public realms were two independent parts. The best architecture in history came about in opposition to these three aberrations. The purpose of this book is to highlight those projects that have sought to contradict these erroneous premises, with the aim to break free from them.

I began this research fifteen years ago, with a number of essays about houses and their repercussions on the environment and on how society is constructed. I was unaware, though, that it would lead me into such an extraordinary world. In fact, the origins of this book go back even further, even less consciously so, when I visited a place that changed my perspective on the work of architects. As I walked through Álvaro Siza's Quinta da Malagueira neighbourhood in Évora, Portugal, which had taken him over two decades to complete, I began to see my profession as a process, as episodes that complement what's already there, a mere medium and instigator of near-imperceptible actions amid the complexity of many people's ongoing lives. I was also profoundly influenced by several visits to the homes of architects: Rudolph M. Schindler in Los Angeles, Alvar Aalto in Helsinki, Walter Gropius in Lincoln (near Boston), Lina Bo Bardi in São Paulo and Luis Barragán in Mexico City. All these houses really draw you in and make you want to stay, but more importantly they also invite you to imagine alternatives to everything that is left outside. Ever since then, I've been intrigued by what happens between a bed and a street; everything between architectural forms and ways of life. Therefore, I've discovered some of the key aspects by studying housing complexes, works that have been taken over by the inhabitants: day by day, these people have to deal with the friction between what is stipulated by the specialists and what the dwellers actually need. In these buildings, it's a slippery slope from coexistence to confrontation. This is particularly evident in Ralph Erskine's Byker Wall in Newcastle, Ricardo Bofill Taller de Arquitectura's Walden 7 near Barcelona, and Elemental's Lo Barnechea units in Santiago de Chile.

Foreword

In housing complexes, you get to see what is merely hinted at between the lines in architecture books. These great communal machines for living are a concentration of the forces that define a society. They encapsulate, more so than anything else, the historic dilemmas concerning the definition of privacy and belonging. Housing complexes contain manifestations of humanity in its rawest state, in a way that cannot be found in any other architectural typology, and only barely depicted in art, film and literature; this is apparent in seemingly circumstantial aspects such as the number of times that residents lock their front door, or the number of apartments with no direct sunlight. These buildings synthesise what lies between the feeling of protection and the state of abandonment, between the need to demarcate one's own territory and the advantages of sharing. They manifest the crossover between utter solitude and extreme overcrowding. The corridors in these complexes are made up of true tales of human existence, of lives trapped between walls and the discourses of architects who have hardly ever lived in such spaces.

The first edition of this book was published in Spanish three years ago, but we are now living in a different world, and architecture must change with an urgency that hasn't been seen for centuries. This calls for a closer look into narratives that favour houses without housekeepers, houses that do not harm the ecosystem or society, houses that consume less, that are more varied and can accommodate more people. Therefore, this new edition is, in many respects, a different book; similarly, we must renew our architecture, it's education, methods of representation, building processes and the ways in which constructions relate to the environment and to people. To create a more inhabitable future, we need to create new forms of existence that might allow us to live *in* the world, rather than living *from* the world. Today, at a time when we know that the planet is reacting to the strain that we put on it, this is a different book because we can no longer keep quiet.

Introduction
Moving from Home

"You can kill a human with an apartment just as well as with an axe."

Heinrich Zille

Looking for a place to live, or designing one, means dealing with contradictory desires: we want privacy in a city-centre location, spaciousness with minimal upkeep, and a place to rest, even if its high cost keeps us up at night. These contradictions stem from the rupture caused by the Industrial Revolution, which divided home and work, countryside and city, and public and private. This split was exacerbated by the capitalist concept of private property, which turned the house into a commodity. In turn, that explains why it's so hard to navigate issues around what belongs to the individual and what belongs to everyone, between resting and inhabiting, between sharing a space and isolating oneself. It also explains why more and more people want to live alone, even if it means building denser housing, ever more separated from nature. What are we really looking for?

These dichotomies can be traced back to the origins of architecture, which emerged when humans built houses to protect themselves from the dangers of the outside world. However, what began as a natural act of defence against a hostile environment led to buildings being cut off from their surroundings. The act of protection thus became synonymous with exclusion: each culture created its own sophisticated mechanisms to decide who and what would be left outside. Decisions were based on religion, politics, health and economics, but almost always in response to irrational fears. As we become increasingly disconnected from our surroundings, there is a greater need to recreate fictitious, idealised environments indoors. Houses have thus become places where people create "a world of their own".

The history of housing is therefore the history of a mismatch between individual desires and communal needs, to such an extent that it is increasingly unclear whether the people inside a house need protection from the environment and those outside, or whether it's the other way round. Moreover, the drawbacks of continuing to build architectures that harm the ecosystem are clearer than ever. There are evident social problems too, with millions of homeless people in the world, and millions of empty houses. And numbers are still going up. So why do we keep on reproducing such harmful models?

To rethink the typology in which we spend most of our lives, most of our money, and which defines our cities, lies in our hands. Looking back over the major changes that have taken place in the history of domestic architecture, we see that the biggest transformations did not begin with sophisticated technological breakthroughs or shifts devised by large firms: they came about when users sought to change some small aspect of their daily lives. For example, the desire to reduce the distance between the sink and the kitchen worktop, to facilitate meal preparation, gave rise to today's modern model kitchen, which is nothing like the simple pot that would hang over the hearth not so long ago. Similarly, out of the need to block the view of a bedroom from the street every time a front door was opened, corridors and foyers were invented to enhance privacy. People's desires inside a house have led to great social and urban transformations, such as childcare being delegated to nurseries, and laundry to dry cleaners. Throughout history, the domestic sphere has been transformed in parallel to our work and socialising habits, which together have led to changes in the ways we eat, dress and rest. For example, the elimination of corseted dresses went hand-in-hand with the transformation of the home, in order to reduce the time dedicated to domestic chores. Likewise, the construction of single-family houses in the "American Dream" suburbs boomed at the same time as car sales and the use of antidepressants. To question an absurdity or a source of discomfort in our daily lives is the first step in reconfiguring the house, along with what defines it: furniture, building systems, forms of communication, cities and people.

In recent years, knowledge about food and medicine — which was previously considered set in stone — has been overhauled. Likewise, we need to rewrite our understanding of the house, so its inhabitants are not compelled to have so many belongings, go into debt, spend the whole day cleaning or live to pay for a space in which they feel trapped. For all these reasons, I propose that we take a closer look at designs that have opened up new ways of interrelating rooms, people and ecosystems.

This book tells the story of modern housing. It is a journey through the major domestic revolutions of the last 200 years, which have aimed to increase privacy without exclusion and overcome the divisions between inside and outside, between home and work and between one neighbour and another. The study follows chronological order, full of overlaps, and it is arranged into five chapters based on the following ideals: freedom, efficiency, wellbeing, identity and coexistence. These chapters explore five aspects for a more liveable future, where the debate on housing becomes the debate on coexistence and equity. This story begins in the early nineteenth century, with the construction of free, modern societies, and it carries into the 2020s, when many of the things that used to be in a house now fit in a smartphone. Furthermore, paradoxically, houses now hold more things, are home to fewer people and are synonymous with confinement. Faced with these contradictions, I reflect not only on architecture but also on the books, exhibitions and films that have sought to lift us out of the mediocre ways in which we inhabit our world.

This book strives to include the work of both architects and inhabitants, and is aimed at all those interested in the different private worlds that have to fit into our common planet. The research stems from my own personal, subjective interests, which I have worked on in parallel to architectural projects that constantly make me question the issues discussed in these pages. The narrative reveals periods when architects started talking about health-related concepts instead of styles, when architectural models were replaced with books on anthropology, and when, a few decades ago, the user ceased to be regarded as an inhabitant and instead became a consumer, a sort of voluntary prisoner. Given that less is not more, bigger is not better, and "fuck context" did not turn out well, I propose a look back on the past in order to reinvent the space upon which our survival depends.

The following five paragraphs briefly explain the contradictions with which we build and inhabit the world. These short anecdotes about how some of the most representative modern architects — namely Frank Lloyd Wright, Le Corbusier, Ludwig Mies van der Rohe, Luis Barragán and Richard Buckminster Fuller — relate to housing, introduce the themes of the book's five chapters. They highlight the incongruencies of residential architecture, which not only affect the lives of individuals but also the definition of a common habitat.

Freedom

Frank Lloyd Wright was born just two years after the abolition of slavery in the United States, at a time when there were no electric lights in houses, no cars and no aeroplanes. His life recounts the transformation of architecture in search of greater freedom. In his efforts to blur the boundaries between indoor and outdoor space, and encourage new forms of coexistence not based on the traditional nuclear family, he fought against the asphyxiating urban densification brought about by the Industrial Revolution. For many years, he worked on designs for a rural utopia called Broadacre City in which each family would have approximately 4,000 m^2 in a kind of open countryside with communal spaces and houses that would not look like fortifications, all interconnected by the latest technology: cars, radios and telephones. Wright's ideal city never actually got built, but many of his beliefs did become a reality, materialised in the two houses where he spent the last twenty years of his life: Taliesin East and Taliesin West, on plots of land each measuring over two million square metres. The houses were physically separated by a 25-hour drive, and they were distinct testing grounds for how to build with different climates, landscapes and wives.

Efficiency

Le Corbusier wanted to build an efficient, technology-based world. He came up with repeatable cells, inserted in structures like bottle racks, as if they were ship cabins taking over a vast urban sea. After devoting his life to thinking about houses as communal machines, he ended up living in an isolated cabin. Le Corbusier needed no more than 3.66 × 3.66 metres of floor space to live in, but with complete privacy, in an almost untouched site on the Mediterranean coast — a far cry from his high-density bottle-rack model. His cabin, which he called his "palace", worked precisely because it was isolated, in front of the sea, a house without a kitchen where his wife had to sleep on the floor, by the sink.[1]

Wellbeing

Mies van der Rohe's architecture embodies the ideal of colonising the world by means of an image of wellbeing, with pristine glass prisms and God in every detail. Mies likened houses to museums and office blocks, in the image of a homogeneous universe built especially for the modern man. However, Edith Farnsworth, the owner of Farnsworth House — the glass "fish tank" designed for her by Mies, and one of the twentieth century's most celebrated works of architecture — said she always felt restless there, like a caged animal on display. She even had to hide away the kitchen bin to prevent it from being seen from every angle, including from the entrance drive.[2] Not even her wardrobe, which served as a partition for the bedroom, fully concealed her while she was getting dressed. Living in a showcase, permanently exposed, was not what Mies wanted for himself. For several years he made a small hotel room his home, and he only personalised the space when he had visitors over, when he would hang up the paintings he otherwise kept under his bed.[3] When Mies was questioned why he chose not to live in one of the Lake Shore apartments he designed, he answered that he'd rather enjoy them from his window than listen to the daily complaints of the neighbours.

Identity

Through his architecture, Luis Barragán sought to express a sense of identity. It was not a matter of reflecting his client's personalities or tastes, but rather evoking his own memories. For Barragán, gardens were the place for personal expression, for the more outrageous ideas that would not suit the indoor space. His own home was the expression of a changing identity, where he lived like a monk in the bedrooms, like a gentleman in the common areas and like a free spirit outside. This was why he thought that houses ought to be gardens, and gardens ought to be houses. Consequently, in his affordable housing projects, the exteriors were designed to be crucial spaces for developing individuality, just as he achieved in the vast paradises he designed for well-off clients. His Ziggurat de Lomas Verdes, a project he imagined for 100,000 inhabitants on the outskirts of Mexico City, followed the logic of *pret-à-porter* fashion: turning *haute couture* into a product that was affordable for all, unique, but also repeatable.

Coexistence

Richard Buckminster Fuller saw the world's population double during his lifetime, and he sought to bring about a befitting coexistence between people and the universe. His struggle began in 1927, when he blamed himself for the death of his three-year-old daughter: as he saw it, he had failed to give her a proper home, free from disease.[4] Fuller was 32 years old at the time, and contemplated suicide, but he lived on to the age of 87, devoted to combining scientific knowledge and architecture. What began as a response to the housing shortage became a life philosophy that sought balance for Spaceship Earth, which he prophetically described as a vessel that has to work for everyone.[5] It took Fuller 65 years to become a homeowner, but when he did, he managed to build it in less than seven hours: a geodesic dome, the strongest and lightest way to cover a space, which he envisioned as pristine. He often insisted that he was decades ahead of his time with notions that later became not only feasible but urgent. That is precisely where we find ourselves today, at a time when ideas that once seemed like something from science fiction have now become possible, and are opening up new alternatives to the unsustainable models that we keep replicating.

These five brief narratives are examples of people who questioned the prevailing models and saw things in their own way. Unlike the chronicles on successful architects with the ability to house the world, these ones provide a glimpse of the crucial factors when it comes to defining ways of inhabiting, even for specialists. They demonstrate that the house is an existential part of the human condition: it is an intimate, personal quest, which at the same time is embedded in a wider shared system.

When we talk about architecture, we rarely address what actually happens inside those spaces, and the analysis of the domestic sphere is no exception: it omits what occurs inside and what is triggered outside. Yet today, in the third decade of the twenty-first century, can't we design better houses than our ancestors? That's why this book revolves around the following three questions: firstly, how can we reinvent the home, taking into account its role as a space that links what belongs to an individual and what belongs to everyone? Secondly, how can we improve ways of living given that we almost always resort to the certainty of past models? And, finally, what are we to do about the fact that a large part of humanity has no house to live in?

The aim of these pages is to bridge the gap between our dreams of inhabiting and the habitats themselves, to seek out alternative housing to live in, and to let live: to revive that wisdom we had as children, when we would imagine a treehouse. For this purpose, I propose to revisit the work of various artists, engineers, homemakers, architects, philosophers, designers and urban planners who have felt the urge to change the way they live, and, in doing so, changed the history of architecture.

---

[1]   See Cid, Daniel and Sala, Teresa M., *Las casas de la vida. Relatos habitados de la modernidad*, Barcelona: Ariel, 2012, p. 145.

[2]   See Barry, Joseph A., "Report on the American Battle Between Good and Bad Modern Houses", *House Beautiful*, no. 95, New York, May 1953, p. 266.

[3]   See Zabalbeascoa, Anatxu and Rodríguez Marcos, Javier, *Vidas construidas, biografías de arquitectos*, Barcelona: Editorial Gustavo Gili, 1998, p. 192.

[4]   See Krausse, Joachim and Lichtenstein, Claude (eds.), *Your Private Sky: R. Buckminster Fuller: The Art of Design Science*, Baden: Lars Müller Publishers, 1999, p. 19.

[5]   See Fuller, Richard Buckminster, *Nine Chains to the Moon*, Philadelphia/New York/London/Toronto: J. B. Lippincott Company, 1938.

Freedom

What is the difference between today's bedrooms, kitchens and dining rooms and those of two centuries ago? Back then, it was normal to sleep in the same area where you ate, and several people would often share the same bed. There were fewer windows, bigger families, more dirt; daily activities were guided by the sunlight, and there was no instant interaction with people on the other side of the world. The lack of adequate climate control in domestic spaces back then is unsurprising, but we are repulsed by the idea of residential buildings without sewage systems. Viewed in this light, we have advanced exponentially. However, despite this progress, there is still a long way to go, especially in terms of sanitation and comfort: today, almost half the world's population still has no running water in their homes. Nevertheless, one essential transformation certainly has led to widespread progress: the desire to achieve, through the house, greater freedom. This ideal spread like never before in the early nineteenth century, driven by a number of political, class and gender-related demands.

    The driving force behind this transformation went far beyond a desire for luxury or comfort: the motivation was to build a free society, based on the idea of housing as a human right, which could lead to the emancipation of residents and spaces. All this emerged at the same time as many movements for self-governance around the world, including the end of slavery in the United States, Latin America's independence from colonial power, the struggles against European monarchies, and social uprisings that demanded rights for the working class. Hygienists, sociologists, gender equality advocates and architects all pushed for new domestic solutions in line with the demands of the time, calling for an end to the logic of the home as a place that enslaves and perpetuates abuse.

    This chapter is structured in four sections. The first one deals with the emancipation of society by means of defending the right to decent housing for all, when, for the first time, architects designed affordable homes for the working class. The second one focuses on open cooperative communes based on the ideals of utopian socialism. The third section looks at the freedom advanced by women through the principles of domestic science, and finally, the fourth section summarises the search for a spatial and formal liberation of the house in the early twentieth century. These four accounts are among the most notable attempts to liberate life through architecture, ranging from minor changes in houses to profound social and political revolutions.

The House as a Right

"Human beings want a home that shelters them without burying them".

Marc-Antoine Laugier

How much freedom can there be in a 40 m² space inhabited by more than three families? At the start of the nineteenth century, most people in the world did not own a house, and many lived in shared rooms. The Industrial Revolution led to overcrowded cities full of makeshift, unsanitary dwellings with no natural light, symbols of a new form of slavery. In Berlin, for example, there was a proliferation of high-density housing estates, the *Mietskasernen*, those "sinister human warehouses". Meanwhile, in New York — dubbed "the city of the homeless" — three-quarters of the inhabitants lived in large housing blocks or tenements, representing a new concept of urban poverty.

The problems related to these houses were generally hidden behind the four walls, but in the first half of the nineteenth century, several publications would change the course of architecture: for the first time, statistics were revealed about the link between infection and squalid housing conditions, and cities were mapped on the basis of health reports, poverty zones and overcrowded housing. These data showed that a large part of social injustice was rooted in the home. Life expectancy in the working-class suburbs, for example, was half that of the middle-class suburbs.[1] As a result, the home became the preeminent focus for bringing about profound social reform.

The first changes took place in London, where industrial development had created problems of overcrowding on an unprecedented scale. Henry Roberts was one of the first housing reformers who strove to liberate the oppressed classes. He designed affordable housing complexes with courtyards, balco-

1 2

nies, ventilation and natural light, more space and a toilet in each apartment. Two of his projects became models worldwide: the 48-flat complex on Streatham Street (London, 1850) [fig. 1], built around a large courtyard with open corridors on each level, and four model homes [fig. 2] for the first Great Exhibition in London in 1851, near Hyde Park.[2] The advantages of these model homes were immediately obvious: economical, good ventilation, individual entrances for each family (via a staircase that opened onto a courtyard at the front), and three-bedroom houses designed to separate parents and children into their own sleeping spaces, and also providing gender-differentiated bedrooms. Until then, the bedrooms were often interconnected, with the circulation routes passing through every room, preventing any possible privacy: Roberts' projects were designed with new values of privacy in mind. His work sparked a movement known as "5% philanthropy", whereby developers agreed to cap their profit at 5% in order to produce better housing for the working class. This led to similar projects initiated by charity groups in Berlin, Amsterdam, Stockholm, New York, Boston and Saint Petersburg.

Another key figure in this field was British social reformer Octavia Hill, who was influenced by her father's interest in penal reform, by her mother's devotion to education, and by her grandfather, one of the first sanitary reformers in London. From the age of 14, Hill worked in a cooperative association managed by her mother, and she assisted her grandfather on several health campaigns. Later, when she was 26, she began to renovate dilapidated houses to help put an end to overcrowding and free tenants from the tyranny of their landlords. Hill's work began in 1864 when she persuaded her friend John Ruskin to fund the renovation of three houses for poor families, in order to provide them with privacy and open spaces outside. In a move against landlords who were interested in their profits, with no concern for the health of their tenants, Hill promoted houses with more than one room, built around gardens, small libraries and spaces for community activities. In a period spanning almost fifty years, Hill improved nearly two thousand homes and started a movement for the preservation of open public spaces.[3] Katherine Square [fig. 3] and Red Cross Garden [fig. 4], two estates that provided small, cheap houses surrounded by gardens, playgrounds and reading corners, are still exemplary today.

In the mid-nineteenth century, two German philosophers, Karl Marx and Friedrich Engels, identified the housing problem as an injustice that was intrinsic to the capitalist model, and impossible to solve through benefit societies that were almost always supported by the aristocrats, the rich or the intellectuals. As Marx put it, "The faster capitalist accumulation takes place, the more miserable the housing situation of the working class",[4] while Engels added "Capital does not want to abolish the housing shortage, even if it could".[5] They both identified the house as a weapon that empowered the privileged classes, and as a system of oppression for the rest of the population. Consequently, in order to ensure basic living conditions, they believed it was necessary to build a new equitable social system and give workers the right to own their homes.

3

This gave rise to various initiatives. One was at the 1889 Universal Exposition in Paris, where, for the first time on an international scale, housing was addressed from a financial and legal standpoint. Furthermore, a series of international conferences on low-cost housing led to the widespread consolidation of affordable housing policies, ensuring regulated rental prices and subsidies to make the technical advances of modernity — running water, electricity and sewage systems — available to all. However, these breakthroughs remained out of reach for many, and often only broadened the gap between different social groups.

At the end of the nineteenth century, a new technology — seemingly unrelated to the domestic realm — led to a fundamental change. Flash photography meant that home interiors could be captured more faithfully than ever before, so deplorable housing conditions were brought to light and made a tangible, irrefutable fact for all, regardless of political ideologies. When Danish émigré Jacob A. Riis arrived in New York, he moved into one of the world's densest slums, the Lower East Side, where he worked as a photojournalist. Riis was one of the first users of flash photography in the United States, and he set out to portray normal life, at day and night, in Manhattan's tenements. Riis published two books, *How the Other Half Lives*[6]

4

and *The Battle with the Slum*,⁷ in which he argued that these slums were an intrinsic part of the city, not a marginal element: "The slum I speak of is our own. We made it."⁸ His books established a link between illiteracy rates, arrests and tenement dwellers: over 80% of criminals lived in deplorable conditions, clear proof that much of the blame for the situation lay with voracious landlords and government inaction. The first pages of *The Battle with the Slum* depicted daily life in the basements, followed by examples of projects that provided some hope: parks with clean playgrounds, swimming pools, paved streets and well-lit areas where people could learn to read for free. His story drew attention to the housing problem, making it a shared responsibility.

    Modernising cities meant demolishing the slums, which led to the affordable housing being built further and further away from city centres, creating endless urban sprawl and then a constant increase in land prices. In Berlin, for example, land prices doubled in fifteen years, and in the Charlottenburg district, they increased five-fold in just one decade.⁹ The house was no longer just a shelter from the elements: it also had to serve as a shelter from the contradictions of the modern world. It had become necessary to leave behind the dichotomies of the new industrial age — between old and new, rural and urban —

and above all, address the inequalities between different types of housing and between social classes. The house had to stop being a symbol of aggression against the landscape and society, and become a key part of the economic, legal and urban structure of the new metropolis.

The transformation of the domestic space into an element of autonomy for modern societies necessarily involved guaranteeing the freedom and prosperity of the residents. To that end, a number of legal initiatives were implemented, including the *Working Class Housing Act* (1890) in England and the *Tenement Blocks Act* (1901) in New York State. The idea behind the latter Act was to stop New York being considered "the city of the living dead". However, in order to achieve these changes, it was not only necessary to bring in new laws that would improve living conditions, but also to re-imagine cities and invent new forms of coexistence and new models for occupying land. They had to be large-scale solutions, and this led to unprecedented urban planning concepts.

One of the founders of modern urban planning, Ildefons Cerdà — the designer of Barcelona's Ensanche district as a prototype for the contemporary city — proposed a sequence of relations between residential buildings, the widths of streets, the modern public transport infrastructure and the new principles of hygiene and freedom. Cerdà established a replicable model of superblocks, where each inhabitant would have 40 m^2 of the city at their disposal, instead of the usual 13.5 m^2 of the time, based on a new relationship between the house and the city. In his famous *General Theory of Urbanization* (1867), he addressed the need to safeguard the freedom of individuals inside their homes, and also in the places between houses: "Independence of the individual in the home, independence of the home in the city, independence of the different types of movement on the city street."[10] A appropriation of the land involved living in freedom at home and moving freely.

Free Communities

"A roof is not the only thing needed to ensure the wellbeing of the masses."

Jean-Baptiste André Godin

In the early nineteenth century, three pioneers of utopian socialism, Henri de Saint-Simon, Robert Owen and Charles Fourier, devised cooperative communities as a way to overcome the incongruity between the defence of individual rights and the decline in the quality of city life. They sought to design new social models that would eliminate the differences between landlords and workers.

Frenchman Charles Fourier was particularly influential. After spending time in prison for rebelling against the government, and being stripped of the wealth he had inherited from his father, he advocated an ideal self-sufficient society housed in a building called the Phalanstery, imagined as a grand hotel and mirroring the layout of the Palace of Versailles. The communal model for this palatial home, for 1,800 people, dispensed with the concepts of family, slavery and repression: everything, both things and passions, would be shared. Fourier, known for having coined the term "feminism", sought to free women from their domestic burdens: the idea was to share cooking duties, leave childcare in the hands of professionals and promote sexual liberation.

Fourier never managed to build his Phalanstery, but after his death, his theories inspired several projects including the North American Phalanx (New Jersey, 1843) and the Familistery (Guise, 1859) [fig. 5] in France. The Familistery, a "social palace", was devised by Jean-Baptiste André Godin, a French worker-turned-entrepreneur who built a cooperative village for 1,200 people in order to improve the quality of life of the workers at his factory. He lived in the complex, which was part of a

5

new social structure designed to ensure better health, education and equality. Godin's employees became partners, and he reinvested the profits into new services for the community, thus giving all the inhabitants of the Familistery equal rights and services.

Godin's Familistery was made up of three residential buildings and a central courtyard, with a library, nursery and shops, laid out like a village square but covered by glass roofs. Unlike Fourier's Phalanstery, the Familistery was based on the traditional family and it encouraged social liberation by means of architectural solutions: bathrooms with running water on each floor, a school, a theatre, a shared laundry, a swimming pool and allotments. The apartments were designed to be customisable, and they ranged from two to six rooms. Godin published his theories in favour of a balance between housing, social and labour structures in *Solutions sociales* (1871).[11] American author Marie Howland, who lived in the Familistery for some time, translated Godin's book into English. Shortly afterwards, she wrote a novel inspired by the community, *Papa's Own Girl* (1874),[12] in which

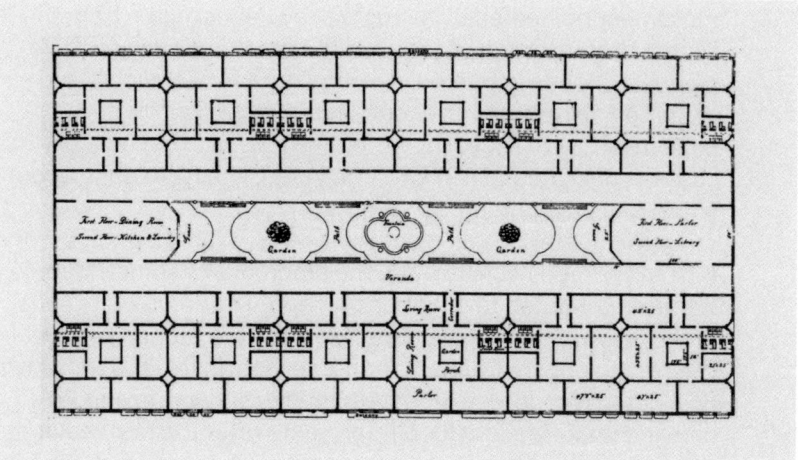

6

she described the advantages of living in this great palace where there was no need for "Cinderella" staff, where communal cooking prevented waste, the buildings had a stable and comfortable temperature inside, and the children were taught by professionals.

The desire to build a fraternal, self-sufficient and free society led Marie Howland to collaborate on one of the most ambitious schemes of utopian socialism: Pacific City, in Topolobampo, Mexico [fig. 6]. The project began in 1886, conceived by civil engineer Albert Kimsey Owen and designed by architect John J. Deery, based on Owen's plans and Howland's advice. It consisted of a regular expandable grid of cooperative housing for a classless society, in a city the size of Manhattan, but without noise or pollution. This model residential estate featured houses with shared services — communal kitchens and laundries, nurseries, shops and libraries — interconnected by parks. The project, which was steered by Howland during the six years that she lived there, was based on cooperation, non-waste and equity. It was also influenced by the Cooperative Housekeeping movement pioneered by Melusina Fay Peirce, again from the United States, who had fostered the creation of cooperative neighbourhoods in Boston. Pacific City was based on the idea of shared ownership. The houses were supposed to be built collectively, with access to hotel-like services.[13] In fact, the city was designed to be like a hotel club, aiming to bring about social and environmental harmony.

Unfortunately, the project grew faster than its services, and it became impossible to quell the ambitions of some inhabitants who wanted to privatise the land. The community split into two groups: those who wanted a private property model that would ensure freedom for the homeowners, and those who advocated a cooperative system as the only way to ensure equity and thus freedom for all. Ten years after the first residents moved in, disputes intensified over the privatisation of not only the land but also the water from a communally-built canal. Owen's 30-year plan soon ground to a halt as a result of these conflicts. Pacific City failed as a cooperative society, and was unable to become "the home of the free". Despite the project's apparent failure, in just two decades the price of the land had increased 633 times. Also, Pacific City helped inspire one of the most influential planning movements of the twentieth century, i.e. the Garden City movement, devised by British town planner Ebenezer Howard.[14]

Historian Lewis Mumford called the Garden City one of the two great inventions of the early twentieth century, alongside the aeroplane: the latter gave humans wings, while the Garden City ensured a better dwelling-place back down on earth.[15] The notion was first posited by Ebenezer Howard, a born inventor who had witnessed the premature death of four of his eight siblings.[16] He travelled to the United States to work for a time as a farmer,where he was inspired by naturalist theories after befriending Henry David Thoreau's mentor, Ralph Waldo Emerson, both of whom championed the essential values of nature. Upon his return to England, Howard published a pamphlet, *To-morrow: A Peaceful Path to Real Reform* (1898),[17] which called for small, self-sufficient communities in harmony with nature, a far cry

7

8

9

from the prevailing industrial system that was choking cities at the time. His idea of "garden cities, social cities" called for shared land ownership and houses with collective services such as communal kitchens, where houses and industries would only be allowed to occupy one-sixth of the land; the rest of the land would be free, in an integrated design that included water supply facilities and public transport. This self-sufficient model, summarised by the slogan, "The City in a Garden", became a reality in the Homesgarth [fig. 7] and Meadow Way Green [fig. 8] complexes of the first garden city in Letchworth (1903). Later on, Guessens Court [fig. 9] was built as part of the second garden city, Welwyn, again founded by Howard on the outskirts of London.[18] The Homesgarth complex, where Howard himself lived, was the culmination of a 25-year experiment, with theories devised by the Cooperative Housekeeping movement: it was based on shared services, cooperation and respecting the land and its resources.

Over time, Howard's cooperative principles were marginalised, and the agricultural zone of his garden city was reduced to a perimeter green belt. The garden-city model that spread around the planet recreated a nostalgic image of the rural world, but left out the project's initial concepts of social and environmental balance. This led to burgeoning suburbs made up of hundreds of houses on private plots surrounded by fenced-off green landscapes. Ever since then, debates on housing have oscillated between two extremes — the dense block of Fourier's Phalanstery, and the sprawling streets of Howard's suburbia — in a distortion of both projects' founding principles, namely cooperative living and equity.

Domestic Revolutions

"The home need be neither a prison, a workhouse, nor a consuming fire."

Charlotte Perkins Gilman

Between the mid-nineteenth and early twentieth century, during the so-called Second Industrial Revolution (or Technological Revolution), a group of women took the notions of productivity, as used in factories, and applied them to the home, in an attempt to liberate domestic life. This movement began in the United States, spearheaded by seven women: Catharine Beecher, Ellen Swallow Richards, Melusina Fay Peirce, Charlotte Perkins Gilman, Lillian Gilbreth, Christine Frederick and Alice Constance Austin. They developed the concept of home economics in order to save time and improve health. Their contributions spanned nine decades, from 1840 to 1930, and in many cases preceded the principles of scientific management devised by American engineer Frederick W. Taylor. The work of these pioneering women led people to question the physical separation between the domestic and public spheres, and the economic distinction between the work done inside and outside the home. The protest movements for abolishing slavery and demanding women's right to vote ran parallel to the campaign for progress in the home.

The transformation of the domestic environment, to permit freer lives, was initiated by Catharine Beecher in *A Treatise on Domestic Economy* (1842).[19] On her many journeys, Beecher took note of the poor health of the women in her country. This was particularly true in the non-slaveholding states, and she realised this was no coincidence: houses themselves enslaved. Beecher detected a link between women's physical ailments and two interrelated sources: poor housing and poor domestic education. She thus began to wage a battle against housing that made people sick, by promoting the science of domestic economy, which she said should be on par with other disciplines like mathematics and physics. Beecher's book listed various health issues — such as problems of posture, skin complaints and lung complications — alongside possible architectural solutions, such as the design of dumbwaiters to transfer food up from the cellar kitchens. It also included instructions on how to prevent infant mortality, which was almost always caused by ignorance about the basics of domestic care. For Beecher, there was no difference between running a house efficiently, ironing a shirt well or providing nutritious food: everything depended on the systematisation of step-by-step processes. Her book was reprinted several times for more than a decade, and it was compulsory reading for generations. It helped make the home and the related domestic activities an object of study.

Catharine Beecher later published *The American Woman's Home* (1869)[20] with her sister, Harriet Beecher Stowe. Three decades separate the two books, and they are markedly different: when the first one was written, houses were built in the Victorian style, typically an amalgamation of several small rooms, but by the time the second book was published, the house had a more open layout, a functional space governed by centralised services, and connected with the community (the neighbourhood, school, church and neighbours). Catharine and Harriet's books played a key role in the emancipation of American society, so much so that when President Abraham Lincoln met Harriet, who also wrote the famous *Uncle Tom's Cabin* (1851), he said to her, "So you are the little woman who wrote the book that started this great war."[21] *The American Woman's Home* was also responsible for another fundamental transformation: the Beecher sisters advocated for an open-plan and repeatable home model, with centralised services.

Ellen Swallow Richards, who was one of the founders of ecology and was the first woman to study at the Massachusetts Institute of Technology (MIT), applied her experience in science laboratories to the domestic realm: she sought to understand the house as a system governed by what went in and what came out of it. Richards was one of the first to study water quality in the United States, and she analysed the amount of arsenic found in wallpaper. At the time, over half the population in cities like Boston were dying before they reached adulthood. This prompted her to pioneer the Home Economics movement and "euthenics", which she defined as the improvement of living conditions. Richards brought advances in chemistry into the home, and she took the kitchen out of the domestic realm and into schools and exhibitions, as a kind of lab for proposing home improvements and bringing down household maintenance costs. Her own house was an experiment in simple living and better health: it had almost no curtains or carpets, natural ventilation entered through strategic apertures, and there was a test kitchen to analyse nutrients and additives in food, and also measure the amount of gas needed to cook different dishes. Richards thought of her home as a model for healthy, hygienic living and cooperation.

In turn, Melusina Fay Peirce — following the premature death of her mother, due to physical exhaustion from excessive housework — founded the Cooperative Housekeeping movement in 1870, in Boston, to call for housework to be remunerated, like any other job. Peirce advocated for the use of communal laundries and houses without kitchens, whereby households would be organised scientifically, and neighbourhoods would be free cooperative societies. She was a central figure in bringing an end to the concept of the home as a completely private space, and thus a private matter, and she fought against inefficient, isolated living. In 1903 she patented the design of a housing block for a cooperative community, and she even wrote a constitution for the new society she'd planned, where there would be no economic distinction between the work done inside and outside the home. Her influence led to cooperative community projects in several parts of the world, although many were suspicious of the urban, political and social transformations implied by these changes to domestic life.

In the early twentieth century, Catharine Beecher's great-niece Charlotte Perkins Gilman sought to change how people think about the home, and the role of women in it. During

Gilman's childhood she moved 19 times in 18 years due to the financial difficulties experienced by her mother, who was separated from Gilman's father. Gilman insisted that women should be freed from the confines of domesticity, so they could earn an income and become independent. She wrote one of the most important books on the impact of houses on society, *The Home, Its Work and Influence* (1903),[22] in which she described humankind's progress in terms of people's relationship with the house. Gilman also questioned its ancient purpose as a defence mechanism against the dangers of the outside world: she believed that people's sense of security should no longer depend on the construction of a solid house, but rather on the construction of a social order that would guarantee the desired stability. That is to say, the home defence system should not be the house itself but the laws of society: the house should stop being a fortress so it can become a place of freedom. Gilman pinpointed the origins of industry in the domestic space — where carpentry, dressmaking, metalwork and pottery all emerged — so the house ought to be considered a vital productive space, just like any other industry. It follows that no industry should waste the time and energy of so many people, i.e. those who would give up their whole lives to domestic labour. She therefore called for the kitchen to be banished from the home, and for domestic work to be made easier and less solitary. This included childcare, which ought to be done in communal spaces with the help of professionals. Given that "home sweet home" did not imply "sweet domestic labour", the relationships between family structures, people's time, finances and belongings needed to be rewritten.

Lillian Gilbreth, one of America's first female Professors of Engineering, studied the relationship between time and movement, which proved to be central to the liberation of home life. Gilbreth brought mechanical organisation into the home in order to improve the efficiency of the spaces and their users. For Gilbreth, as a mother of twelve children, bringing industrial advancements into the home was a matter of basic survival.[23] For example, she designed an L-shaped kitchen, and she proposed a "work triangle" that would cut the distance between the stove, refrigerator and sink (she reduced the steps required to bake a cake by five-sixths, from 281 to 45). Fewer steps meant less fatigue, and more freedom. Gilbreth brought together administrative science and psychology: she was a pioneer in ergonomic studies, pursuing a harmonious relationship between household objects and bodies, and she also brought to light the link between chronic illnesses and poor architectural design. The layout of a space has real, physical effects, and acknowledging this completely changed the perception of design, which had previously been underestimated.

Christine Frederick, a teacher turned mother and housewife, would listen to her husband's business discussions while she sewed clothes, and she became interested in the new notions of scientific management on the basis of Taylorian logic. If a bricklayer could lay three times as many bricks by following the emerging science of labour efficiency, what might happen if the same approach were applied to the housework that consumed so much of women's time, day and night? Frederick turned her kitchen — where she spent more than 70% of her time — into a kind of laboratory for her experiments, in an attempt to simplify every single task.[24] In *The New Housekeeping* (1913)[25] she pointed out the absurdity of supposed domestic solutions, almost always invented by people who did not actually use the things they designed or sold. At a time when food accounted for 40% of household expenditure, Frederick emphasised the urgent need to redefine the household as a factory: food, furniture and products were not just created spontaneously by users, but rather they should be considered part of a new system of production and consumption.[26] The economic impact of good housekeeping would bring more freedom and a better future to families and industries everywhere.

These ideas for a new approach to organising time and resources began to take hold around the world. In 1901, German activist Lily Braun published a theoretical treatise on the centralisation of domestic labour, which influenced several housing projects in Europe that were built with communal

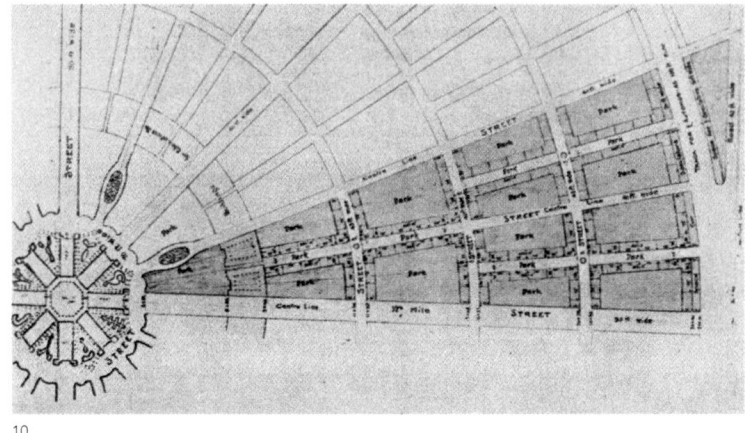

10

kitchens.[27] In France, Paulette Bernège denounced the time wasted due to bad domestic practices (the time spent by ten million people on domestic labour in France totalled an annual loss equivalent to 65% of the country's wealth).[28] Paradoxically, these ideas emerged while many still questioned the feasibility of installing toilets in the home. Adolf Loos, for example, claimed that a bathroom was too expensive, and that a single sink was enough for a whole family to wash themselves, their clothes and also for use in cooking.[29] In small houses, it was still common for the cooking area to be a multi-purpose area: it would double-up as a space for other kinds of work, as well as bathing and even sleeping. Meanwhile, in large houses, the kitchen was often located in dark basements, with few (if any) windows. As women became more actively involved in the conversation, there was a complete rethink of the domestic space, in the interests of greater freedom.

The project that best illustrates the desire to free peoples' lives through their houses was Llano del Rio (California, 1915) [fig. 10], designed by Alice Constance Austin. This project, which was never built due to financial problems and a lack of water, consisted of houses with parks and collective services. The houses would be connected by tunnels for a heating system and waste disposal, and through which electric railcars would deliver food and products. Austin encouraged the future inhabitants to have a say in the design of their homes, and she called for a reorganisation of the community's work to ensure less wasted time and more freedom. To that end, the houses would be connected to a central kitchen providing meals for a thousand families, and managed by ten professional chefs, instead of building a thousand kitchens run by a thousand amateur cooks. To achieve this, the house would have to adapt to the working logic of its services. Austin was concerned that nearly half the population had to prepare 1,095 meals every year in the course of a lifetime, as well as having to clean up afterwards. In 1935, she published *The Next Step*,[30] a critique of the disconnect between the mechanical and the manual, work and family, and between countryside and industry. The book included details of her Llano del Rio project with its houses, green roofs, civic centres, parks and communal kitchens, in an urban system designed to reduce waste. The book's preface provides a good character profile of Austin and her fellow forerunners of domestic engineering, with their "minds of an engineer, the common sense of a housewife, the spirit of Joan of Arc, and the imagination of a poet".[31]

During the early decades of the twentieth century, the world's first women to ever study architecture and design helped reduce the burden of domestic life, allowing greater freedom. The work of European women such as Lilly Reich, Eileen Gray, Margarete Schütte-Lihotzky and Charlotte Perriand provided a more comprehensive account of the relation between materials, devices, activities and spaces. Schütte-Lihotzky, Austria's first female architect, designed the "Frankfurt kitchen" (1926), a modular kitchen installed in thousands of homes with a very clear argument: "A typical kitchen needs twice the space to do a tenth of the work."[32] Schütte-Lihotzky developed her kitchen as a model of mass production and spatial simplification. Her efforts did not stop at redefining domestic interiors: she also worked on the design of houses that could be extended in the future, as well as self-built temporary homes for transitory rural immigrants. Like the other examples mentioned in this section, rethinking the house meant rethinking the relationship between space, furniture and social roles, and above all, it meant pushing the boundaries of the concept of freedom.

Spatial Freedom

"The house has been dissected into its plastic elements. The static axis of the old construction has been destroyed."

Theo van Doesburg

In the early twentieth century, several architects — influenced by avant-garde art — tried to do away with the idea of the house as a closed box, synonymous with oppressive space. The emergence of reinforced concrete and metal structures made it possible to obviate load-bearing walls, so there no longer had to be repetitive divisions between floors. Designers could now imagine open-plan layouts on each floor, with flowing spaces and thus more dynamic lifestyles. This trend is well illustrated by four projects from the 1920s that came up with new ways of liberating people's spaces and lives: Rudolph M. Schindler's Schindler-Chace house; the Rietveld-Schröder house designed by Gerrit Th. Rietveld and Truus Schröder; Eileen Gray's E-1027 house; and Frank Lloyd Wright's Ocatilla Desert Camp. All four designs advocated new lifestyles and transgressed the boundaries of the established concept of the family. Their creators, all born in the second half of the nineteenth century and almost all of whom were self-taught (only Schindler had a degree in architecture), are hard to categorise, precisely because each one took a different route in this quest for greater freedom.

Schindler built the Schindler-Chace House (Los Angeles, 1922) [fig. 11] to create an open setting for two couples (namely his own and the Chaces). After camping for several weeks in the Yosemite National Park, he embarked on this project with the idea of replicating the sense of freedom that he had experienced there, with regards to the advantages of sharing ser-

11

vices, activities and views. The house, a wooden construction influenced by traditional Japanese architecture, was designed for four independent adults — and their children, later on — and was based on a sequence of independent spaces around gardens. These spaces were not assigned any specific activity (kitchen, living room, bedrooms, etc.). Instead, the activities themselves defined the use of each space: rather than designing rooms, he proposed open-air "bedroom baskets" on the roof. Fireplaces, place both inside and outside, were the only elements that defined the otherwise free spaces. Each adult had a kind of apartment room for working and living an informal life, somewhat like camping. Years beforehand, in Vienna, the young Schindler had been a disciple of Adolf Loos, who taught him to consider spaces as free sequences on the basis of Loos's *Raumplan*, and thus mould his architecture to the body's desires.

The Schindler-Chace house is a pretty disorientating place. It does not follow an ordinary domestic layout, but is rather a sequence of rooms with no predetermined purpose, the result of Schindler's questioning of the sense of belonging, privacy, relations with the public realm and the established concept of marriage and family. More than a house, it was a kind of avant-garde cultural centre where concerts, performances and political meetings were held. It was also Schindler's studio, and several different people lived there over the years, since one section was rented out as an apartment. Some years later, the Schindlers separated, but then shared the house as a divorced couple, where at times they communicated exclusively by letter. According to critic Reyner Banham, "Schindler designed this house as if there had never been houses before. It marked a fresh start for architecture."[33]

The quest for freedom from static, conventional architecture was influenced by the artistic vanguards — Futurism, De Stijl, Constructivism, Neo-Plasticism, Cubism and Dada — as well as film, photography and Albert Einstein's theories on the relativity of time. What mattered in the design of a house was the expression of movement, the space-time experience and a new concept of freedom based on change. In Cubism, the human body became an elusive, mobile, fragmented organism; meanwhile, the architectural space became the representation of a flowing environment with no distinction between inside and outside, between above and below. Like Pablo Picasso's paintings of distorted faces with simultaneous frontal and profile perspectives, the house became a set of concurrent independent elements within a single space. The founders of Dutch Neoplasticism — Piet Mondrian, Theo van Doesburg and architects J. J. P. Oud, Cornelis van Eesteren and Gerrit Th. Rietveld — favoured a "new total environment" without boundaries between different disciplines. This collaboration between painters and architects gave rise to houses that broke free from spatial rigidity. In 1923, Van Doesburg and Van Eesteren designed several houses for an exhibition, *Les architectes du group "de Stijl"*, held at the Galerie L'Effort Moderne in Paris. Using models and drawings, they emphasised the independence of the basic building components — walls, floors and foundations — in a free, loose layout. Although these projects were never built, they exemplified the attempt to move beyond the stifling nature of houses, do away with axial symmetry and make space flexible. This led to a major shift away from architecture considered as a closed container, perforated by a few small windows, to a three-dimensional space composed of infinite relations between lines, spaces and voids. The search for spatial freedom, based on the principles of the De Stijl group, was materialised in the Rietveld-Schröder house (Utrecht, 1924), built by Rietveld together with the owner, Truus Schröder, with whom he also collaborated on other works. The Rietveld-Schröder house had movable partitions and multipurpose spaces. The windows, ceilings and furniture formed a changing organism that was even used by Rietveld himself as a studio for some time.

Eileen Gray's E-1027 house on the French Riviera (Roquebrune-Cap-Martin, 1929) [fig. 12], designed in collaboration with her partner, publisher Jean Badovici, also used sliding panels, rotating elements and furniture built into the spaces. During the construction process, Gray spent long periods on site; she took note of the sun's trajectory and the direction of the winds for nearly three years, in order to include intuitive gestures and the changing conditions. That is, the spontaneous process of appropriation, of making the house one's own, would inform the design. She designed nearly a hundred items for the house — including lamps, screens, rugs and door handles — to free up how the space is used.[34] Although it was a small and austere house, it had a music corner, one kitchen for winter and another for summer, a workshop for guests, an outdoor bed, versatile tables and windows with adjustable apertures that challenged the vision of one-way functionality. Gray, who defined the house as "the extension of the human being, their liberation, their spiritual emancipation",[35] believed that every house, no matter how small, should allow its user to feel totally independent. This concept is visible in the next house Gray designed for herself, Tempe à Pailla (Castellar, 1932), a place to spend some time alone, to escape, and at the same time, to find herself.

Frank Lloyd Wright, throughout his career, challenged the closed nature of the bourgeois home by building spaces that stretched out to the horizon in every direction, reflecting the freedom of the American Midwest's vast landscape. He wanted to break down the house-as-cube, and instead create flowing spaces that could take the domestic realm beyond its walled boundaries. This logic led him to build the Prairie Houses, based on the following principles: "To eliminate the room as a box and the house as another by making all walls enclosing screens [...], and so the whole more liveable. Liberal is the best word."[36] His ideals on freedom are summed up in the Ocatilla Desert Camp, Arizona (1929): spatial fluidity and architecture reduced to its minimum, in harmony with the surroundings, thus enabling a way of living without the usual trappings. Wright designed this campsite in an afternoon: it would be somewhere he could live and work for a season, along with his family and a group of students in a communal adventure. They built it together in just over a month, using timber and canvas, to achieve versatility and good ventilation. Wright drew upon Henry David Thoreau's ideas about the quest for freedom and being in contact with nature; in this campsite, Wright wanted to design his own version of the archetypical primitive dwelling, based on the notion that different human groups live in different ways, such as a cave or a hut or a tent. That is, he sought to look beyond the clichéd log cabin that Thoreau had built for himself in a forest on the shores of Walden Pond, near Boston, by then a legend in historical debates. And so it was that Wright built his own Walden in the form of a tent. Its nomadic character allowed for greater freedom, and unlike Thoreau, he did not live in it alone, but communally. Wright regarded this temporary structure as the building model for a democratic society, a representation of architecture as a free organism. When they left the camp for the winter, the local Navajos dismantled it and reused the material in their own buildings, according to the logic of total flexibility.

Perhaps unsurprisingly, the Ocatilla Desert Camp bears a conceptual resemblance to the house built by Schindler, who

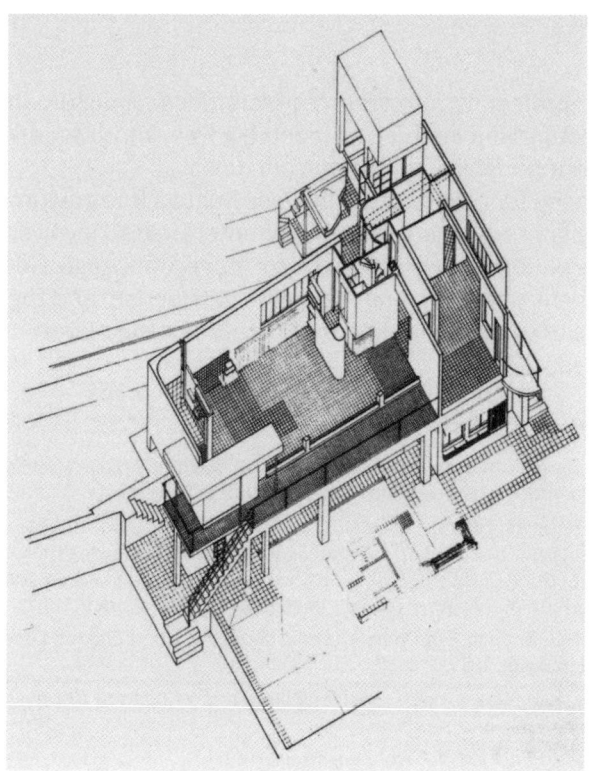

12

worked with Wright for two years. Ocatilla brings to mind the image of camping and a sailboat, a reference to a life of change and in communion with nature. One of the three chapters in Wright's autobiography is devoted to freedom, and in that chapter the project he describes in most detail is precisely Ocatilla, created instinctively with lightweight materials in direct relation to the place: "Unqualified to build, we are still busy making caves for cave-dweller survivals [...]. I now felt more than ever oppressed by the thought of the opaque solid overhead of the much too heavy mid-western house."[37] He therefore suggested, "So, rather than ponderous blunders [...] why not ephemera?"[38]

For this project, Wright erased all reference to monumental architecture and instead, advocated a free, improvised, more active relationship with the surroundings.

In these four examples of houses built as free environments, the designers were also the inhabitants. They all involved experimentation with space and form, based on usage. However, the difficulty of balancing the desire for freedom and the constraints of everyday reality would pre-empt the main architectural debates in the following decades.

---

[1] See Bauer, Catherine K., *Modern Housing*, Boston/New York: Houghton Mifflin Company/The Riverside Press Cambridge, 1934, p. 20.

[2] See Roberts, Henry, *The Dwellings of the Labouring Classes, Their Arrangement and Construction*, London: The Society for Improving the Conditions of the Labouring Classes, 1850. After the houses were dismantled at the end of the exhibition, they were reassembled in Kennington Park in 1852.

[3] See Hill, Octavia, *Our Common Land, and Other Short Essays*, London: Macmillian & Co., 1877.

[4] Marx, Karl, *Das Kapital* [1867] (English version: *Capital: A Critique of Political Economy*).

[5] Engels, Friedrich, *Zur Wohnungsfrage* [1887].

[6] Riis, Jacob A., *How the Other Half Lives: Studies among the Tenements of New York*, New York: Charles Scribner's Sons, 1890.

[7] Riis, Jacob A., *The Battle with the Slum*, New York: The Macmillan Company, 1902.

[8] Ibid., p. 9.

[9] Bauer, Catherine K., *op. cit.*, p. 25.

[10] Cerdà, Ildefons, *Teoría general de la urbanización*, Madrid: Imprenta Española, 1867, vol. I, p. 3 (English version: *General Theory of Urbanization*, Barcelona: Actar, 2018).

[11] Godin, Jean-Baptiste André, *Solutions sociales*, Brussels: A. Le Chevalier Éditeur, 1871.

[12] Howland, Marie, *Papa's Own Girl*, New York: John P. Jewett, 1874.

[13] See Owen, Albert K., *Integral Co-operation: At Work*, New York: John W. Lovell Co., 1890.

[14] See Ortega Noriega, Sergio, *El Edén subvertido. La colonización de Topolobambo 1886-1896,* Mexico City: Instituto Nacional de Arte e Historia/Secretaría de Educación Pública, 1978, pp. 180 and 206.

[15] Mumford, Lewis, "The Garden City Idea and Modern Planning", prologue to the 4th edition of Howard, Ebenezer, *Garden Cities of To-Morrow*, London: Faber & Faber, 1960.

[16] See Williams, Karl, "Geoists in History, Ebenezer Howard (1850-1928)", *Progress*, Winter 2020, p. 26.

[17] Howard, Ebenezer, *To-morrow. A Peaceful Path to Real Reform*, London: Swan Sonnenschein & Co., 1898; published in 1902 as *Garden Cities of To-morrow*.

[18] Homesgarth (1909) and Guessens Court (1922) were designed by H. Clapham Lander, and Meadow Way Green (1915-1924) by Courtenay M. Crickmer. Letchworth was designed by Howard's understudies, Raymond Unwin and Barry Parker, and Welwyn by Louis de Soissons.

[19] Beecher, Catharine, *A Treatise on Domestic Economy, for the Use of Young Ladies at Home and at School*, New York: Harper & Brothers, 1842.

[20] Beecher, Catharine and Beecher Stowe, Harriet, *The American Woman's Home: or, Principles of Domestic Science*, New York: J. B. Ford & Co., 1869.

[21] O'Neill, Helen, "Birthplace of Harriet Beecher Stowe for sale for $ 1", *Kalamazoo Gazette*, Kalamazoo, 21 October 1997, p. D6.

[22] Gilman, Charlotte Perkins, *The Home, Its Work and Influence*, New York: McClure, Phillips, & Co., 1903.

[23] Two of her offspring described this logic, which they experienced at home, in: Gilbreth, Frank B. Jr. and Gilbreth Carey, Ernestine, *Cheaper by the Dozen*, London: William Heinemann, 1948.

[24] See Frederick, Christine, *Meals That Cook Themselves and Cut the Costs*, New Haven: The Sentinel Manufacturing Co., 1915.

[25] Frederick, Christine, *The New Housekeeping. Efficiency Studies in Home Management,* Garden City: Doubleday, Page & Co., 1913.

[26] See Frederick, Christine, *Selling Mrs. Consumer*, New York: The Business Burse, 1929.

[27] See Braun, Lily, *Frauenarbeit und Hauswirtschaft*, Berlin: Verlag Expedition der Buchhandlung Vorwärts, 1901.

[28] See Dumont, Marie-Jeanne, "If Women Made Houses: Paulette Bernège's Crusade", in Fromonot, Francoise; Didelon, Valéry and Chabard, Pierre (eds.), *Yours Critically, Writings on Architecture from Criticat Issues 1-10*, Paris: Criticat, 2016.

[29] Loos, Adolf, "Die moderne Siedlung", *Für Bauplatz und Werkstatt*, Stuttgart, January 1927.

[30] Austin, Alice Constance, *The Next Step. How to Plan for Beauty, Comfort, and Peace with Great Savings Effected by the Reduction of Waste*, Los Angeles: The Institute Press, 1935.

[31] Ibid., Preface by Edgcumb Pinchon.

[32] Kirsch, Karin, *The Weissenhofsiedlung: Experimental Housing Built for the Deutscher Werkbund Stuttgart, 1927*, New York: Rizzoli, 1989, p. 26.

33 See Banham, Reyner, "The Master Builders: 5" [1971], in Banham, Mary; Lyall, Sutherland; Price, Cedric and Barker, Paul (eds.), *A Critic Writes: Essays by Reyner Banham*, Los Angeles: University of California Press, 1999, p. 172.

34 See the Introduction to: Wang, Wilfred and Adam, Peter (eds.), *E.1027, Eileen Gray*, Tübingen: The University of Texas at Austin/Ernst J. Wasmuth Verlag, 2017.

35 Adam, Peter, *Eileen Gray, Her Life and Work*, Munich: Schrimer/Mosel, 2014, p. 134.

36 Wright, Frank Lloyd, *Modern Architecture*, *Being the Kahn Lectures for 1930*, Princeton: Princeton University Press, 1931, p. 74.

37 Wright, Frank Lloyd, *An Autobiography* [1932], New York: Rizzoli, 1994.

38 Ibid.

Efficiency

Our lives are constantly being defined in terms of efficiency, i.e. the relation between time, cost and results. Nature has taught us so much in this regard: for years, we have been learning about plants that extract the maximum nutrients using the minimum energy, and about the regenerative nature of cells, forests and the entire universe. In this context, "efficiency" means getting what we want with minimal resources — and, ideally, with a minimum amount of waste. In nature, there is no notion of waste, which is one of the great lessons we have still not taken on board. Doing the maximum with the minimum is different to knowing how to make the best, intelligent use of what we have. Thinking about efficiency in the short term is not the same as thinking about it in the long term: the former often precludes the latter, since there are always other factors at play: money, time, CO_2, waste… and lives. Ever since the dawn of humanity, we have tried to make our spaces and building systems as efficient as possible. However, our priorities have changed enormously: efficient for whom, and at what cost?

This chapter looks at ideas that aimed to improve the performance of the components that define a shared habitat, from minimal repeatable cells to large-scale city infrastructure. It includes the search for potential savings according to an "economy of urgency", enabled by technological development and by finding more efficient ways of living together. The chapter focuses on the early decades of the twentieth century, especially the interwar period: during this period, great efforts were made to link architecture with industrial progress, in order to build affordable housing on a large scale; homes were built with a logic similar to that of car manufacturing; and houses were designed to be sold by catalogue and delivered by mail. Architecture was based on standardised systems and new engineering processes. In this context, designing a house not only entailed imagining a domestic sphere for a family, but it was also about creating productive societies and functional cities.

The following five sections define this quest. The first one looks at the creation of houses as efficient mass-produced machines, and the efforts to determine their optimal grouping; the second section is about utopian urban projects, based on a mechanical relationship between the house and the city; the third one analyses designs for efficient sharing; the fourth is about prefab housing; and the final section deals with vertical housing. All five sections reflect a shift in focus during this period: architects began looking at technical, financial and planning logics too. That is, they were designing not only spaces, but also systems and replicable models, in an aim to control the effectiveness of a house on the basis of its weight and its use of resources and services. The common denominator of the proposals in this chapter is how they attempted to provide more affordable and useful housing for more people: the idea was to improve the productivity of the building industry, and thus improve spaces, cities and their users.

Machines for Living

"The minimum subsistence dwelling has to simultaneously become a new form of life."

Sigfried Giedion

After World War I (1914-18), solving the housing shortage meant reconstructing — with scarce resources — houses, towns and also the collective memory. The Great War had disrupted the economy, health and the make-up of families, which now included an unprecedented number of single people, childless couples and single-parent families. In Europe, this led to the construction of new, efficient houses, based on industrial production, as a way to heal society and rebuild cities. The concept of efficiency — as developed by the pioneers of domestic science, discussed in the previous section — was not readily applicable to the classical Victorian house: it required better-equipped dwellings, closely connected to public services. The layout and plumbing of a house not only affected each aspect of everyday life, but also determined a new logic of urban planning. Architects became responsible for connecting the small domestic scale with the wider urban dimension; this was the basis for the emergence of the modern movement, in an unprecedented attempt to solve, efficiently, the matter of human habitation. This new trend derived from four initiatives which envisioned the house as a repeatable ideal model: 1) the renewal of the domestic space based on the concept of "machines for living"; 2) a new school, the Bauhaus; 3) the Weissenhofsiedlung, a housing exhibition in Stuttgart; and 4) a series of international congresses, the CIAM.

During this period, architecture had fallen behind other industries, to an alarming extent. Le Corbusier thus proposed the construction of industrialised houses that were just as efficient as

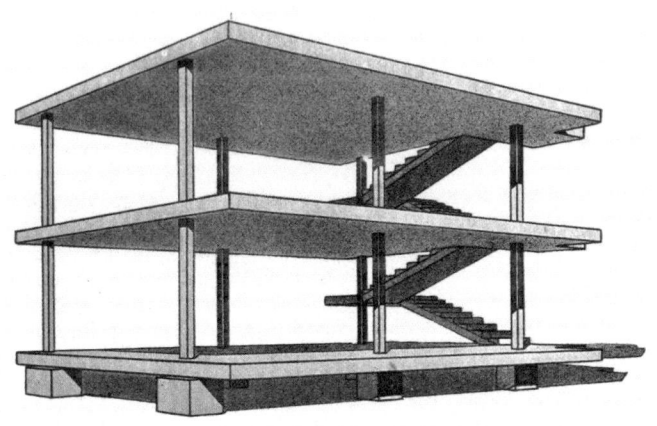

13

technological devices, i.e. houses "as practical as a typewriter".[1] With this logic, he designed the Dom-Ino House (1914) [fig. 13], a simple reinforced concrete structure on a 6 × 9-metre floor plan, a repeatable system for rebuilding the world. He wanted to design a universal house that would use the most efficient building method, and which could be adapted to suit the varied requirements of different inhabitants. Mass-producing houses would not only increase productivity, but it would also encourage a new moral value: standardised components would establish a balance between the homes of the poor and the homes of the rich.

The Dom-Ino House was promoted as a standardised frame with interchangeable parts, as if it were a car. The cost of producing one car in 1904 was the same as that of producing six cars in 1924, and yet, over that same period, the cost of housing went up.[2] Therefore, Le Corbusier aimed to follow the logic of industrial efficiency developed in the USA by engineer Frederick W. Taylor and car manufacturer Henry Ford, who claimed that it should be possible to change house as quickly as one changed clothes.[3] While Taylorism was concerned with systematising labour, Fordism was about popularising products and making them accessible to the

14

middle class. In other words, it was not enough to improve workers' performance — they had to be turned into consumers. In just fifteen years, from 1914 to 1929, the number of cars in the United States increased from 2 to 26 million.[4] Accordingly, for architecture to become attainable for everyone, the obsolete production processes would have to be dusted down and transferred to clean factories, as part of the logic of the newly invented cash registers. Also, crucially, it would mean propagating a new spirit: for Le Corbusier, dissemination and raising awareness was just as important as the design solutions themselves. With all this in mind, Le Corbusier advocated a new kind of home science, *domism*, which he equated with the science of the city, *urbanism*, and the engineer was heralded as the new hero of the age. According to Le Corbusier, when we talk about mass-producing houses, we should really be talking about creating common services. His ideas about the house as a communal machine for living are summarised in L'Immueble-villa (1922) [fig. 14], a block of 120 apartments with shared amenities — kitchen, sports facilities and central gardens — that encouraged a healthy life for all, not unlike Charles Fourier's Phalanstery. Le Corbusier envisioned the Immueble-villa as a new system of share-based joint ownership. Although the project was never built, one Immueble-villa unit did see the light in the Pavillon de l'Esprit Nouveau at the 1925 International Exhibition of Modern Decorative and Industrial Arts in Paris.

The crux of the idea was to stop considering the house as an individual dream, and instead regard it as a mass response. The efficiency of cabins on ocean liners and trains was studied: the living quarters themselves were reduced to a minimum, but this was offset by larger spaces for shared activities, such as joint dining rooms and common areas. A key aspect in this regard was the influence of the "aparthotel" buildings in Chicago and New York, built in the late nineteenth and early twentieth century. These 10 to 20-storey residential buildings, equipped with hotel-like amenities, could accommodate up to 4,000 residents, and served as their workplace and hub for social life. Three such buildings in Manhattan — the Waldorf Astoria, the Plaza and the Ansonia — exemplified this new idea of a residential hotel that subverted the usual living dynamics: in these buildings, the rooms, technology, centralised domestic services and public life were all interconnected. The Waldorf Astoria's main lounge, Peacock Alley, for example, was used by thousands of people every day.

The condominium-hotels were run like factories: the centralised services, kitchens and laundries were similar to assembly lines, with specialised employees working on specific tasks. These urban machines for living were a showcase for all sorts of innovations, including the first flush toilets, pneumatic tubes for sending messages and small items from one room to another, and room service for in-room dining, thus applying the revised notion of efficiency to day-to-day life. The Ansonia had a rooftop allotment with cattle and hens, so that, every morning, a butler could deliver fresh milk and eggs to the apartments. The Waldorf Astoria even had its own internal railway for VIP guests. But how could the benefits of these gigantic machines — which so deftly combined privacy in the apartments, the efficiency of shared services and the hubbub of public life — be placed within the reach of the everyday citizen?

The challenge was to find optimal solutions for building systems, for urban planning and the interior layout of homes. The architect's work therefore had to range from "the cushions on the sofa to the construction of cities".[5] At that time, talking about a house meant talking about mass-produced neighbourhoods; architects thus had to focus their efforts on defining the new parameters of affordable housing, with a view to managing how cities would expand. Walter Gropius founded the Bauhaus school in 1919, influenced by the Deutscher Werkbund. The Bauhaus was where the architectural foundations for industrialised mass production — as well as the standardisation of house components — were first put forward. What better place than the home to test the connection between small-scale and the urban scale, between manual and mechanical, object and space?

The new rational formulae for housing were disseminated at the *Die Wohnung* [The Dwelling] exhibition on the Weissenhofsiedlung estate (Stuttgart, 1927), a showcase of houses in a new workers' colony built by the Deutscher Werkbund under the direction of Mies van der Rohe. The exhibition included 63 houses designed by some of the leading architects of the time, including Walter Gropius, Le Corbusier, J. J. P. Oud, Bruno Taut, Ludwig Hilberseimer and Peter Behrens. The houses showed off the new forms, materials and construction systems that had been designed to maximise usable space, while also offering greater flexibility, better ventilation and more sunlight, at a reduced cost and in less time. The entire complex was constructed in about five months; in fact, Gropius's two dwellings took less than three months, using prefab components. Mies built a 24-unit block with a metal structure and flexible interiors [fig. 15] that surprised observers with its construction speed and interior flexibility. For this project he worked in collaboration with Lilly Reich, and he also consulted Erna Meyer, a Doctor of Economics, who promoted the lessons of the female domestic reformers. One of the apartment interiors was designed by Reich, who from then on collaborated on Mies's most emblematic works: she highlighted the adaptability of spaces thanks to new material possibilities.

The Weissenhofsiedlung was a catalogue of the new architectural language, but it fell short as a model for affordable housing for communal living. Most of the houses were sin-

15

gle-family dwellings, and they were neither particularly cheap nor small: some of them had five or more rooms, and many included servants' quarters. The public complained that certain materials and elements were simply out of reach of the working class: the large windows, for example, would be hard to clean, cold in winter and hot in summer.

In the following year, 1928, the International Congress on Modern Architecture (CIAM) was inaugurated in Switzerland by Le Corbusier, Ernst May, Sigfried Giedion and Hannes Meyer, among others. The aim of the Congress was to define the concept of modern housing, and address how to make it affordable for the majority. Traditional craft building methods therefore had to be replaced. Since the first CIAM, these architects stressed the importance of architectural education, starting at primary school: those new generations would become the future buyers of modern houses, and they would soon consider it normal to see doors of a uniform size, installed all over the world, and the standardisation of bathroom designs or entire construction systems. Standard norms for housing solutions had been established as a result of the Amsterdam Housing Congress (1918): spaciousness, efficiency and good insulation could be applied to houses all over the world. For example, to qualify for public funding in Frankfurt, the standards defined by the city ordinances had to be met. Also, the optimised prototypes for bathrooms and kitchens, developed by Margarete Schütte-Lihotzky, were put into use thousands of times.

The intention at the time was to turn the work of architects into an almost scientific task that spanned everything from determining the optimum window dimensions to detailing how the spaces were really used, including by outsiders like the postman and the neighbours. The private space thus ceased to be an issue that concerned solely its users, and became a quantifiable system that could undergo universal improvements: the house was now subject to public control. Several studies by Alexander Klein, a Berlin city-planning advisor, summarised the methods for achieving "clean" layouts so that no one family member would hinder the movements of the others. The intention was to create, in Klein's words, "functional houses for frictionless living",[6] i.e., houses that would ensure efficient, uncluttered lives. The analogy of the house as a heavy antique chest gave way to a modern lightweight suitcase, intelligently arranged into compartments.[7] A room's size in square metres became less important than its width, its orientation, its different possible furniture layouts and other aspects previously considered intangible such as shade, conduciveness to rest and the flexibility of the spaces. The smaller the house, the higher the price per square metre, so it was pointless trying to compress them any further. Instead, the key was to make homes more adaptable, with multi-purpose spaces, moveable partitions, communal services and mixed uses. In order to maximise the available space, furniture became an inseparable part of the domestic environment: benches and walls were adapted so they could store things, and rooftops were converted into multi-purpose terraces. These were all part of a new kind of living environment that was both systematised and customisable.

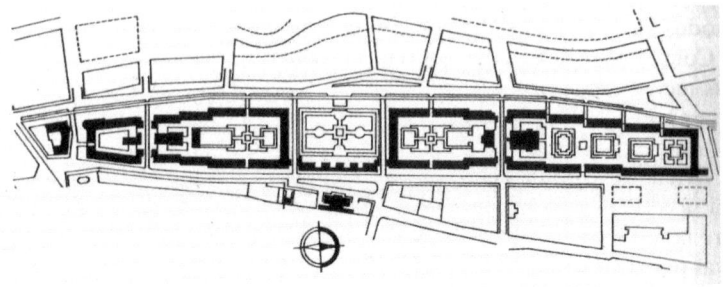

16

The second International Congress, CIAM II, was held in 1929 in Frankfurt under the theme *Die Wohnung für das Existenzminimum* [The Dwelling for Minimal Existence], with the aim of determining a more efficient way to organise the home. The Congress arose in opposition to the detached single-family house, and focused on the German *Siedlungen* and the *Höfe* in Red Vienna, built at a time when architects Bruno Taut and Martin Wagner were working for the public administration in Berlin, as well as Ernst May in Frankfurt and Adolf Loos in Vienna.[8] Implementing the new standards in terms of living spaces and urban quality meant that architects had to get involved in politics. Karl Ehn's Karl Marx-Hof complex (Vienna, 1927) [fig. 16] exemplifies this tendency. It had 1,382 dwellings with communal services such as a library, a health centre, a nursery, a communal laundry, shops and playgrounds. This monument to the proletariat freed up almost 80% of the site, providing green spaces and making this communal housing project look truly colossal, with a façade that was over a kilometre long.[9] Suddenly, architects were not just designing houses or apartment buildings, but defining an actual social order and tackling entire portions of new cities. The Dammerstock housing estate (Karlsruhe, 1929) [fig. 17], designed by Walter Gropius and others, shows what can happen when architects collaborate.[10] Dam-

17

merstock is a set of 228 dwellings with 23 different types, with apartment blocks, terraced houses and recreation areas. This was a new model, designed to make the most of the sunlight and the green areas.

The priority during this period was to establish the minimum necessary living conditions. However, when experts tried to define the minimum amount of space, light, air and heat needed by human beings to live decently, they found it was impossible to set common values across different geographical regions and needs. Therefore, not only was it necessary to solve the housing shortage using limited resources, but also the solutions had to suit different customs and climates. This issue became all the more obvious when new representatives joined CIAM II, including Alvar Aalto from Finland, Josep Lluís Sert from Spain and Richard Neutra from the USA. At this Congress, Le Corbusier defended the value of regional housing like the Russian *izba* and the Vietnamese thatched hut, and pointed out the need to apply this age-old wisdom in every corner of the planet. However, one crucial question remained: how could these personal and regional demands possibly be addressed amid the severe post-war housing shortage, when the only feasible solution was an industrial-scale approach in order to multiply housing prototypes millions of times?

The House as City

"Through the organisation of individual rooms in the floor plan, the functional building that encompasses an entire street block is born."

Ludwig Hilberseimer

The desire to build an orderly new world, for a renewed society, arose in the 1920s and 1930s: cities would be designed from scratch, as if they were huge blank canvases. The idea was to get rid of the house as an irregular element, shaped by the multiplication of individual desires, and instead turn it into the base unit of a large-scale universal plan, using efficient formulae to determine population density, solar orientation and percentages of open areas and circulation routes. Four utopian cities reflect the underlying principles of these reproducible, repeatable worlds, guided by an almost mechanical relationship between the house and the city; the aim was to extend the concept of design accuracy from the smallest cell all the way up to the entire city, and beyond.

Le Corbusier's Contemporary City of Three Million People (1922) [fig. 18] took his mass-production logic to the extreme. It called for run-down historic districts to be levelled and replaced by skyscrapers, thus forming much more densely-populated cities. Almost all of the remaining land would be left free for gardens, in a world with efficient circulation: it would be like his Dom-Ino House, but rather than a system for individual cells, it would be extended in order to build miles upon miles of houses.

Ludwig Hilberseimer's Vertical City (1924) [fig. 19] combined two types of cities in one compact solution: an upper, residential city with pedestrian circulation, and a lower city for commerce and work, with roads and subway lines. It was a critique

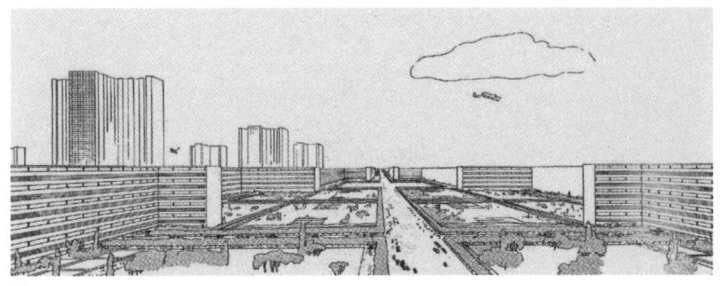
18

19

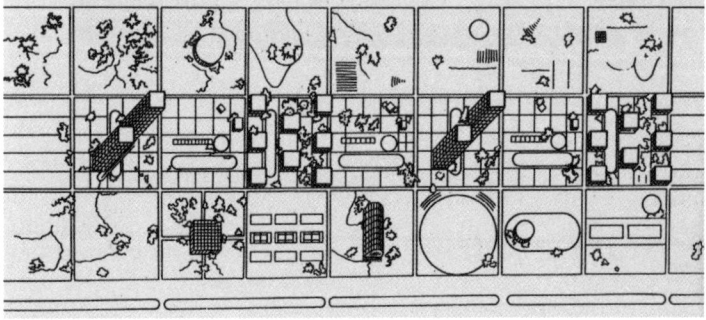
20

Efficiency

of Le Corbusier's Contemporary City, its fictitious density and the foreseeable congestion problems when going up and down the towers. Against this, Hilberseimer advocated for the construction of residential spaces above a commercial city. He proclaimed the death of the private house, which he blamed for spreading chaos in cities, and he proposed communal houses that would cover an entire block so that people could live above their workplace, while also minimising traffic and limiting the horizontal sprawl of cities. Houses would be designed with the same logic as the hotel, including rooms perfectly equipped with built-in furniture, and all the amenities that the city could offer. This Vertical City championed the simplification of housework, the end of traffic and a detachment from belongings: "When moving to a new apartment, one no longer has to pack the moving van, but only one's suitcase."[11]

The Magnitogorsk project (1930) [fig. 20], designed by the members of the OSA (Organisation of Contemporary Architects) under the leadership of Ivan Leonidov, emerged as the model city of Soviet socialism. The design consisted of a linear city following a chequerboard pattern, made up of small collective communities in which work, leisure, education and agriculture were all interconnected. These neighbourhoods, with communal houses, residential units and shared dining rooms, were to be surrounded by gardens, pools and sports facilities, dispensing with the need to create rest homes outside the city. Around the perimeter, main highways limit the city, conceived as a narrow carpet, 25 km long, stretching across the land to connect industrial hubs. The city was defined by a series of glass residential towers, decades ahead of the ones built in Chicago and New York.[12] The idea behind the Magnitogorsk project was to level out the differences between country and city, and also between work, houses and recreational spaces.

The final example, Frank Lloyd Wright's Broadacre City (1932) [fig. 21], opposed the verticality of large centralised cities, which exacerbated the inequity of a society divided between owners and tenants. Wright was one of the first modern architects who tried to solve the problem of low-income rental housing. In the late nineteenth century, he began to design communal housing that redefined the tenement paradigm, with economical resources, spatial generosity and openness towards the exterior. Forty years later, he went even further with his Broadacre City. This project was not about housing design, but rather a decentralised form of urban development in which each family would have a minimum of four thousand square metres, instead of the usual 10 m^2 per person.[13] Wright proposed a synthesis of the rural and the urban, the private and the communal: "No private ownership of public needs [...]. No public ownership of private needs."[14]

Wright's project was based on organic horizontal growth, in contrast with Le Corbusier, Hilberseimer and Leonidov, who instead came up with orthogonal city grids starting with the very precise design of the housing unit, which was then scaled up to the block and the city, forming a synthetic relationship between the different parts. Despite the differences between their projects, all four architects focused less on the design of houses and cities and more on the design of a method. In each case, the architecture defined a system, an abstraction: these were cities drawn on blank sheets of paper for model inhabitants, as a way to respond ideally and efficiently to the pressing issues of modern living.

Shared Lives

"[The new house] is primarily a social enterprise because, like every DIN standard, it is the standardised industrial product of a nameless group of inventors."

Hannes Meyer

The most radical examples of efficient rationalised housing were developed in the Soviet Union, in line with socialist ideals: after the Revolution of 1917, the right to private property was abolished. A key point of reference is the photograph of Swiss architect Hannes Meyer's Co-op Interieur (1924) [fig. 22]. This image of a room is a manifesto for a classless society in which everyone would have the bare minimum. The most interesting thing about this photo is not the extent to which a room can be pared back — cells in prisons and monasteries have been like this for centuries — but rather that it highlights the importance of the collective services that make such reduced living spaces feasible. This model of tiny, near-empty rooms works precisely because of its interconnection with communal spaces. Meyer published the picture of the Co-op Interieur in 1926, in his manifesto "Die neue Welt" [The New World], in which he insisted on the logic of cooperation as the only way to humanise the massive scale of industrialised processes. The room could only be designed as a minimal element if it were part of a complex equation of shared services. Efficiency did not necessarily mean the minimum, but rather the most connected, the best served. This, he claimed, was the only way to rid oneself of practically everything, but not of other people, nor the exterior.

The Co-op Interieur was just one of Meyer's various Co-op projects. The Co-op Theatre, for example, consisted of plays for which he created the scenes, the costumes and the script, as a kind of propaganda manifesto about cooperative lifestyles. The

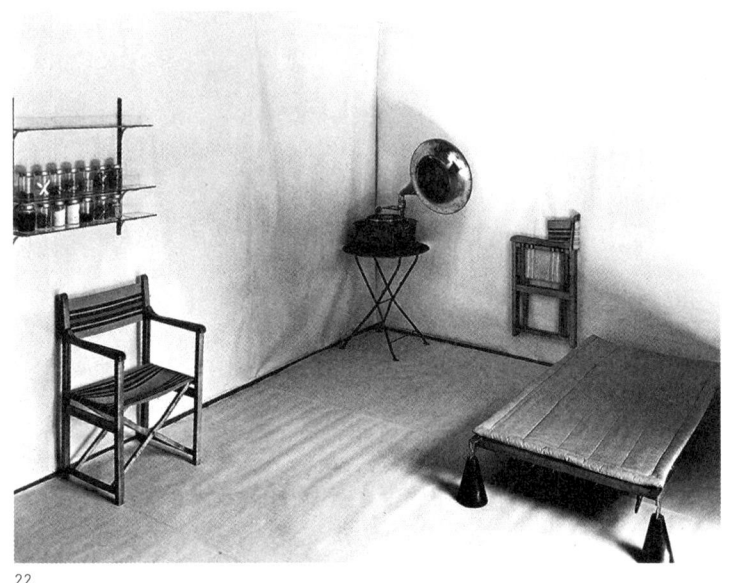

22

use of puppets acentuated the differences between the human and the artificial, between the communitarian and the individualistic. Meyer's architectural and theatrical discourse aimed to show that the human social condition would only be feasible if collectivity and a sense of humility could take precedence in all people's lifestyles.

This logic also took shape in Karel Teige's explorations for minimal houses. In Teige's view, cities had become concentration camps for the proletariat, where the "machines for living" were nothing but a representation of the "machines of splendour" of a technical luxury that was out of reach of the majority.[15] Teige proposed a standardised architecture, created cooperatively by architects, economists, labourers, doctors and politicians, to guarantee houses where people of different ages, sexes and social classes could live together in kitchenless apartments with communal spaces, and without class or gender divisions. His book *The Minimum Dwelling* was a radical manifesto about the possibilities of communal living.[16] Against the micro apartment of the *Existenzminimum*, Teige sought to link the individual cell with the collective spaces and centralised services; this way, unpaid work could be replaced by the mechanisation of domestic chores, and the socialisation of caregiving services would be put in the hands of professionals.

The ideas about the socialist living environment were based on Friedrich Engels' theories, which had been published almost half a century beforehand. Soviet workers' cooperatives required a new mentality: "We don't need English cottages. We don't need individual apartments. Provide a complete house where the working-class family can live, where it can inter-relate with other families, meet in a common room [...]. We constantly talk about a new way of life, yet we lock the worker in his apartment. That solution does not suit us."[17] The logic of cooperativism led architects to rethink the concept of the house in an attempt to set a new social balance, and eliminate the differences between industry and the countryside. In architecture, the individual client was replaced by the "social recipient", and collective blocks — with an area of 6 × 9 metres per person, and adjacent communal services — were designed, as part of a community life filled with shared facilities.[18]

Some of the pioneers in Europe's housing transformation, including Hannes Meyer, Ludwig Hilberseimer, Bruno Taut, Ernst May and Margarete Schütte-Lihotzky, soon moved to the Soviet Union. For almost a decade, the projects were characterised by their opposition to single-family houses, which were described as "individual cages". As an alternative, the collectivisation of spaces and domestic labour was favoured instead. The designs aimed to break down the traditional living concept of families: there were communal dormitories, with separate buildings for adults and children; the adults would not sleep with their partners, and the children would receive professional training from an early age, separated from their parents.

23

This new communal model is exemplified in the Narkomfin Building (Moscow, 1929) [fig. 23], a block of 57 flats built by Moisei Ginzburg and Ignaty Milinis as a "social condenser", in keeping with the social ideology of Ginzburg's OSA Group. Narkomfin had a communal dining room, a gym, a library, and several types of housing, from minimal one-room cells to three-room duplexes that offered different typologies for different family models. The intention was to enable a gradual transition from the traditional models to the new principles for collective living. Ginzburg himself lived in Narkomfin, and he designed several interconnected levels (the corridors only occupied two of the building's five floors) to improve efficiency, provide more natural light and make the most of the corridors as open, symbolic places for social congregation. When Le Corbusier visited Moscow, he studied the section of Narkomfin, and 20 years later, it was a source of inspiration for his Unité d'Habitation in Marseilles. The Narkomfin Building reflected the transformation of Soviet socialist ideals over the years: a penthouse for a high-ranking government official was built on the shared roof; the free plan (on pilotis) was taken up by various additions; the dwellings were subdivided; and the common service areas stopped working.

The Soviet communal housing experiment only lasted a few years due to political changes that took place in the USSR, and before long, the communes became a fiction. The reality was quite different: uncomfortable places with little living space, where residents had to line up to use the dining rooms and bathrooms. Between 1923 and 1933, the designated living area per person was reduced by 25%,[19] and in the 1930s, under the slogan "communalised life", it was further reduced from an average of 4 to 1.7 m^2 per person in extreme cases, while building costs per square metre had dropped by 50%.[20] The shortage of services, the lack of privacy and the resulting degradation led to this model being questioned. The logic of sharing degenerated into a restrictive act, where efficiency was confused with repetition. An erroneous interpretation of the statistics and excessive political control were the reasons why individual needs and the true meaning of the collective were ultimately forgotten in subsequent projects.

Houses by Mail

"Men will always rebel against attempts at over-mechanization which is contrary to life. But industrialization will not stop at the threshold of building."

Walter Gropius

In the first few decades of the twentieth century, prefabricated construction systems were designed: repeatable houses could now be built, with unprecedented savings. The United States became the leading developer of prefab housing thanks to its technical capacity and its efficient transportation network, which facilitated the distribution of products. The country's enormous size made it difficult to build centralised housing projects in the same way as in Europe, so mass repetition emerged as the best solution.

Sears-Roedbuck, a company which started out selling small objects by mail-order catalogue, soon became an emporium supplying an essentially rural society, otherwise disconnected, with products ranging from cars to houses. In thirty years, Sears sold over 100,000 prefabricated houses, in nearly 500 different designs.[21] In the Sears catalogue (*The Modern Houses Program*), modernity was manifested in the distribution, construction and assembly systems, although not in the architectural forms or their spatial layout. Like other companies that sold houses by catalogue, the important thing was efficient production and the potential for market growth; this led to a boom in portable houses, including homes on wheels, which in turn contributed to greater population dispersion in the United States after 1935. However, these homes on wheels were not really within the architects' remit, and most of them were also far removed from the basic notion of the home.

Prefab housing was enriched by the experimental work of four pioneers — Frank Lloyd Wright, Richard Buckminster Fuller, Walter Gropius and Jean Prouvé — who designed repeatable, flexible building systems. For nearly four decades, Wright designed houses as sets of components; Fuller devoted his life to expanding the potential of prefab houses; Gropius worked on creating a system of prefab homes from the outset of his career; and, for several decades, Prouvé built "demountable" houses (i.e. houses that can be taken apart and reassembled). Although none of the projects designed by these architects were ultimately reproduced on a mass scale, they offered further potential solutions to the shortage of millions of homes in an immediate, economical and attractive way.

Wright designed economical homes with modular construction systems that were adaptable, which is crucial for a country like the United States where there are totally different climate zones. The initial construction systems were made from wood, and later from concrete blocks. He devised the American Ready-Cut System (1915-17) which featured modular timber components based on the traditional balloon frame method and Japanese architecture. The logic was like that of the Froebel wooden-block toy set that his mother had given him when he was a child, and with which he discovered the infinite possibilities of combining basic forms. In just two years, Wright produced nearly a thousand drawings of houses that could be assembled with this system, but the hundreds of models he patented never made it to the production line.

In the 1920s, Wright devised the Textile Block System, using cast concrete blocks for the different parts of a house, i.e. the walls, trusses, pillars, etc. He used this system to build four houses in California, including La Miniatura (Pasadena, 1923), but it proved laborious and expensive (La Miniatura ran over the initial budget by 70%). In the decade following the 1929 financial crash, Wright designed the Usonian houses, based on a modular grid he called the Unit System, and using prefab

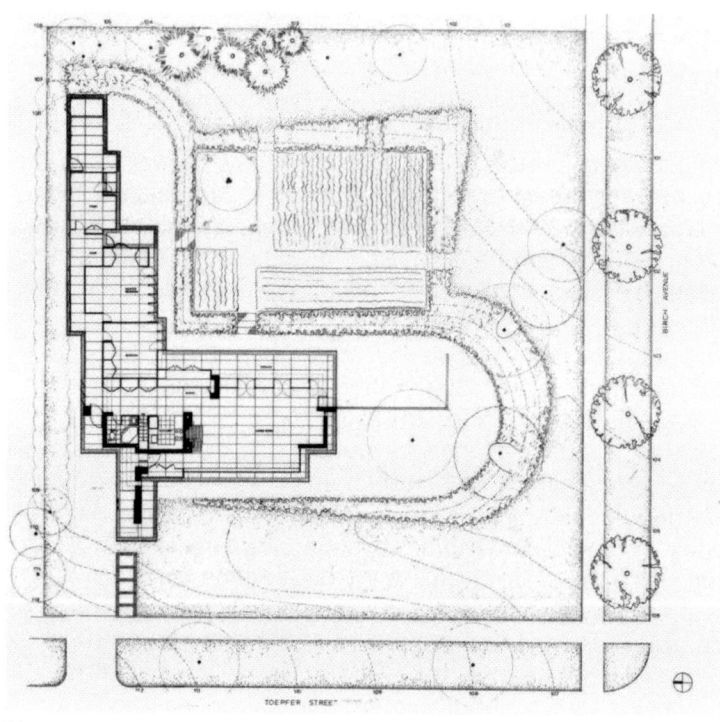

24

plywood panels. The best example of this approach was the Jacobs I House (Madison, 1937) [fig. 24], built in less than six months, and notable for its spatial richness and bioclimatic efficiency. Wright used the same system to build nearly 30 houses, but his plans were cut short by World War II. He kept on developing this system until his 90s, trying to come up with an efficient model that would allow infinite flexibility. However, he was unable to produce it on a mass scale.

Buckminster Fuller designed several prefab home prototypes, trying to create the most efficient assembly system. He began his research in 1927, inspired by the construction of the Graf Zeppelin, the biggest airship in history: he sought to take the tensile systems, used in aeronautics, and apply them to architecture. In the same year, the young, self-educated Fuller published his ideas in a manual/manifesto titled *4D Timelock*.[22] A year later, he designed 4D House, which could be built in one day, and 4D Tower House, which contained houses with no walls, stacked around a service core, with a membrane similar to the ones used in zeppelins. Fuller envisioned the house as an autonomous, soundproof, self-cleaning unit, with pneumatic doors and built-in furniture that could be entirely transported by air. He claimed that his ideas were 25 years ahead of their time. Clients asked him for a house, and Fuller "offered them an entire industry".[23] Later on, the 4D House was renamed the Dymaxion House [fig. 25], a dwelling that brought cutting-edge technology into architecture, and designed to reuse resources.

In the 1940s, Fuller built a new version of this prototype. The Wichita House was a circular metal shell, inspired by the mechanisms used in umbrellas and bicycle wheel rims. It was easy to assemble, with efficient fixtures, and a revolving natural ventilation system in the roof that prevented dust from entering. The house could be cleaned effortlessly in one hour: it was a sterile space for a new lifestyle, as well-controlled as its shell. Fuller defended the need for lightweight, portable houses: the weight of the Wichita House was just 1% of that of the average dwelling, and any individual part of the structure could be carried by one person with one hand. Furthermore, the house's components could fit into a cylindrical container, allowing eight houses to be loaded onto a single railway wagon. Fuller was responsible for bringing into the architectural debate the issues of mobility and reducing energy consumption in homes.

Fuller built two samples of the Dymaxion House, but refused to market this prototype because he felt it was still incomplete. He thus continued to develop his ideas for the Dymaxion Deployment Unit (DDU), of which more than 1,000 units were built in a single year, for worldwide distribution. As he saw it, the problem of human housing was a problem of efficiency in terms of services and storage. This led him to devise the Autonomous

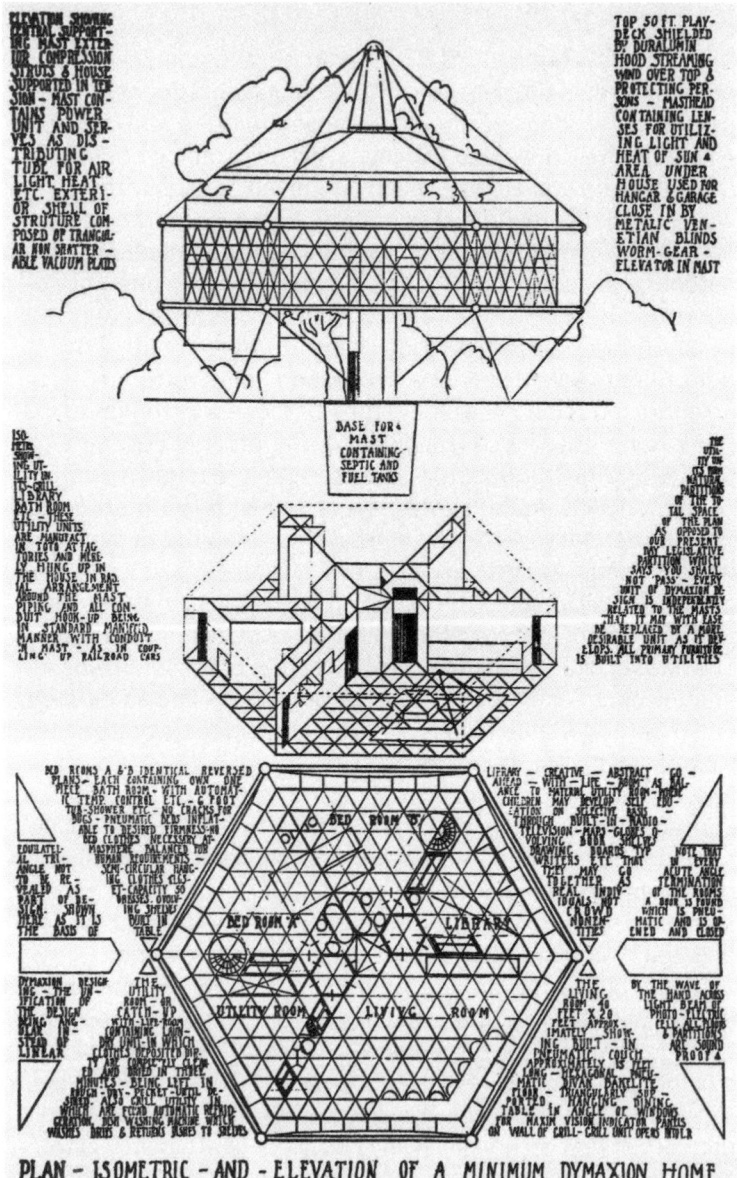

PLAN - ISOMETRIC - AND - ELEVATION OF A MINIMUM DYMAXION HOME

Package N1-N16, a portable container with all the necessary interior components of a house — chairs, bathroom, kitchen and accessories — that could save owners 90% on household products. He also devised an integral bathroom (the Dymaxion bathroom), an aluminium monoblock, and a trailer home (The Mechanical Wing). The Wing was a unit with a kitchen, bathroom and a device to attach it to the car: any corner of the world could be turned into a liveable space.

One of Fuller's greatest contributions was to consider the inhabitant as an active part in the assembly of the house, and the house as a finished, instant package. He believed that technological innovation should not be used for military purposes, but rather to improve standards of living. He shared Le Corbusier's idea of the house as a machine for living, but he regarded it as a living mechanism, a changing organism, hence his avoidance of concrete. The distinction between the two architects was sharply explained by Fuller himself: "In architecture, "form" is a noun; in industry, "form" is a verb."[24] His goal was to cover the largest amount of space with the least amount of material, which would base the value of a house on its weight ($1/lb, or $0.50/kg in the case of the Dymaxion house) and its efficient assembly (the Wichita house was designed to take one day and six workers to erect; the DDU, six days and two inexperienced workers).[25] Although he received orders for these prototypes from all over the world, only a few models were actually built, and his dream of mass production never really came true.

Walter Gropius drafted the theoretical basis for mass-produced housing components in 1910, when he was working at Peter Behrens' studio in Berlin. This marked the start of an initiative that would occupy him for almost four decades. In the 1920s, Gropius devised the Baukasten system with Adolf Meyer; in the early 1930s, he built copper houses using prefab components; later, in the 1940s, after fleeing to the USA from Nazi Germany, he designed the Packaged House with his colleague Konrad Wachsmann. This project aimed to make the most of the latest American technology and reverse the trend that had seen the cost of cars in the United States fall by 60% between 1913 and 1937, while the cost of houses increased by 193%.[26] The Packaged House was the peak in terms of designs for a universal prefab housing system. Gropius and Wachsmann wanted to use a lightweight plywood system for different types of houses, with standard components that were easy to transport and suitable for any climate. The most innovative feature of their system was the four-way panel connector, devised by Wachsmann to facilitate on-site assembly of walls and floors, depending on individual desires (the first prototype was built in a single day with the help of five non-specialists). The idea was to create a whole new building industry based on this system, but it proved incompatible with other standardised components (such as doors and windows) that were beginning to appear on the market. This was compounded by a chain of financial crises in the late 1940s and various bureaucratic hurdles that slowed down the system's production. Ultimately, only 200 of these houses were built, and like Wright and Fuller's systems, each invention posed unexpected challenges. When the copper versions were exported to Tel Aviv, for example, the copper panels proved to be worth more than the buildings themselves: the houses were dismantled so the panels could be melted down and sold.

Jean Prouvé built prefabricated houses in France for more than two decades. He believed that the solution was to bridge the gap between designer and manufacturer, so he stepped into the role of both. He applied the rules of Meccano building sets to house construction, and he produced over 200 draft designs and nearly 30 prototypes which were used to build over 800 houses, from shelters for war refugees to exportable homes. Some were made of timber, others were made of aluminium, but they were all part of a lighter approach to construction: it would have lesser impact on the land, using ready-to-assemble components for the most efficient modulation. Prouvé was, along with Fuller, one of the first designers to manufacture a complete, finished bathroom in a factory. He wanted to make architecture an affordable, variable industrial product: "The dress you bought last year is different from the one you'll buy this year. It's an industrial product [...]. This year's house will be different from the one built next year."[27]

It all began in 1937, with the desire to build economical, "demountable" houses. The French government passed a law on the right to paid holidays for employees, but the vast majority could not afford to go away somewhere. So, Prouvé designed the 3.3 × 3.3-metre BLPS demountable metal house, which could be assembled in less than four hours. The outbreak of the Second World War, two years later, cut short his plans. Nevertheless, he employed the same logic in the design of a prototype for demountable barracks for twelve soldiers that could be erected in three hours, but its mass production was halted once again due to financial problems. In the 1940s, he worked with Pierre Jeanneret on the design of the BCC prefab demountable metal house, and he went on to build 450 demountable homes.

Additionally, Prouvé designed the Métropole houses built from components that could be lifted by two people and assembled in three days. They were meant to last a generation, and they are, in fact, still being used today. Prouvé's aim was not to put up houses using prefab components, but to produce entirely factory-built houses that required no further additions. In this time, he also designed the aluminium Tropical House, which five workers could assemble in five hours, with a ventilated lattice façade for the hot African climate. One of these prototypes was exported to Nigeria and two to the Congo (as it used to be called), but the locals received them as colonialist objects made from aluminium extracted from their own land, which was then taken to France for processing and returned in the form of objects that flaunted their makers' technological superiority. The fate of Prouvé's projects was very different from what he envisioned: "Our buildings form a whole; we are equipped to make entire complexes, not fragments of houses."[28]

The market was not ready to embrace the inventions designed by Prouvé, Wright, Fuller and Gropius, but their projects opened up new building and spatial possibilities. Part of the problem was that they had to be produced in large numbers to make the venture profitable, and the builders' unions opposed the changes, fearing job losses as a result of this do-it-yourself logic. A further complication was the fact that, after World War II, aerospace companies entered the housing sector with economical models that were very hard to compete with. Unfortunately, the future of the prefab house was left in the hands of commercial manufacturers who were not particularly interested in architecture.

Vertical Houses

"Is a reasonable development of the city conceivable if all its citizens live in single homes with gardens?"

Walter Gropius

In the 1930s, the use of lifts, metal structures and reinforced concrete led to the proliferation of designs for apartment towers, offering an alternative to the inefficient horizontal expansion of cities. The debates on housing focused on issues related to density and the concentration of services. Walter Gropius, for example, highlighted the need for highrise construction because of the time wasted on commuting: in Berlin, this time was estimated to be two full years of each employee's lifetime, assuming a 30-year working life.[29] Likewise, Le Corbusier pointed out the advantages of vertical densification by quantifying the huge number and lenghts of streets, drains and infrastructural elements required for detached single-family houses.

The construction of high-rise apartment blocks entailed a new way of thinking about services, streets and circulation. The small gardens in single-family homes were replaced by large, communal green zones around these towers, which called for a rethink about the size of the street blocks and the design of these open spaces. As a result, a new approach to urban planning became necessary: the car was the protagonist, so traffic would have to be separated from the houses, and pavements replaced by squares. Also, public space would no longer be regarded as a mere extension of the street, but rather as a new, large open space between highrise towers. Setting standards, in this regard, thus became crucial: these specifications would dictate the width of the streets, the size of the space between buildings, and the minimum percentage of open space on each plot.

CIAM III, the third congress in the series, held in Brussels in 1930, focused on "Rational Site Planning" as a way to find the most effective solutions for the subdivision of land, orientation and building height. The aim was to test whether orderly housing design would automatically give rise to orderly cities. The debate on how best to cluster dense apartment blocks led to CIAM IV, held in Athens in 1933, which addressed new urban models under the theme "The Functional City". For the CIAM participants, the city was no longer the home of human beings, since it could no longer satisfy the fundamental needs of its inhabitants. This led to *The Athens Charter*,[30] which defined the guidelines for the construction of the efficient metropolis of the future: cities with segregated housing blocks, set back from the street and raised on pilotis to guarantee sunlight, fresh air and silence. Green spaces thus began to be considered as the key ingredient for habitability. They were important not only because they were accessible outdoor areas, but also because of their significance as a public space, fostering collectivity and an element of shared property. Under this new logic, the main attribute of this kind of housing was the democratisation of the open space between the buildings.

The Athens Charter called for distances between the home and the workplace to be reduced to a minimum, and for private interests to be subordinated to the common good. However, the attempts to organise the city by its different functions led to a physical division of life into home, work, leisure and commuting. Houses ended up becoming mere dormitories, cut off from everything else, largely because the freestanding apartment blocks were in fact conducive to the rise of the car as a central feature of modern life. Henry Ford had endorsed the construction of housing estates far from the city centre, where residents would invariably need cars — that is, the cars that Ford himself was manufacturing. Over time, though, this model came in for harsh criticism, so much so that a new approach to architecture and town planning emerged: it called into question the principles of the modern movement, the limitations of urban density and the very concept of efficiency. Could something be efficient without being comfortable, or be useful without producing shared wellbeing? At this point, designers began to understand that people needed cities that not only worked better, but that worked for everyone.

---

[1]   Le Corbusier, *Vers une architecture*, Paris: Èditions G. Crès, 1923 (English version: *Towards a New Architecture*, New York: Dover Publications, 1986, p. 240).

[2]   See Yorke, F. R. S., *The Modern House*, London: Architectural Press, 1934, p. 167.

[3]   Henry Ford, quoted in a 1929 interview by A. M. Smith, in Giedion, Sigfried, *Befreites Wohnen*, Zurich/Leipzig: Orell Füssli Verlag, 1929, p. 43.

[4]   See Rowe, Peter G., *Modernity and Housing*, Cambridge (Mass.): The MIT Press, 1995, p. 10.

[5]   Various authors, *100 años de arquitectura y diseño en Alemania 1907-2017, Deutscher Werkbund*, Munich/Stuttgart: Architektur Museum Technische Universität München/IFA, 2008, p. 13.

[6]   Klein, Alexander, *Vivienda mínima: 1906-1957*, Barcelona: Editorial Gustavo Gili, 1980.

[7]   The publication of Ernst Neufert's *Bauentwurfslehre* (*Architects' Data*, 1936), was a milestone in this regard.

[8]   In Berlin, Martin Wagner headed the municipal technical office, Bruno Taut was building director and Alexander Klein housing construction advisor. Ernst May headed the social housing policy of the Weimar Republic, Adolf Loos was head of the town planning department in Vienna, and J. J. P. Oud was chief architect in Rotterdam.

[9]   A decade earlier, in 1917, 73% of Vienna's housing was in deplorable condition. However, when it passed into the hands of municipal management, housing was built with services and green areas, and rental prices dropped from 25% of the working-class salary to 2%. See Tafuri, Manfredo

and Dal Co, Francesco, *Architettura Contemporanea*, Milan: Electa, 1976, p. 191 (English version: *Modern Architecture*, New York: Rizzoli, 1986).

[10] Otto Haesler, Wilhelm Riphahn and Franz Roeckle all worked on Dammerstock.

[11] Hilberseimer, Ludwig, *Grosztadt Architektur*, Stuttgart: Verlag Julius Hoffman, 1927 (English version: *Metropolisarchitecture and Selected Essays*, New York: GSAPP Books, 2012).

[12] See *IAUS*, 8 (*Ivan Leonidov*), New York, 1981, p. 20.

[13] See Wright, Frank Lloyd, *The Disappearing City*, New York: William Farquhar Payson, 1932, p. 17.

[14] Wright, Frank Lloyd, *The Living City*, New York: Horizon Press, 1958, plan on back cover.

[15] See Teige, Karel, *Nejmensi byt*, Prague: Václav Petr, 1932.

[16] Ibid.

[17] Aymonino, Carlo, *L'abitazione razionale: atti dei congressi CIAM, 1929-1930*, Padua: Marsilio, 1973.

[18] Lisitsky, El, *1929. La reconstrucción de la arquitectura en la URSS y otros escritos*, Barcelona: Editorial Gustavo Gili, 1970, p. 186.

[19] Aymonino, Carlo, *op., cit,* pp. 78-91.

[20] See Khmelnitsky, Dmitry, "Moisej Ginzburg and Soviet Residential Architecture", in Udovički-Selb, Danilo (ed.), *Narkomfin, Moisej J. Ginzburg, Ignatij F. Milinis*, Austin: The University of Texas, 2015.

[21] See Terrados Cepeda, Francisco Javier, *Prefabricación ligera de viviendas. Nuevas premisas*, Seville: Universidad de Sevilla, 2012, p. 216.

[22] Fuller, Richard Buckminster, *4-D Timelock*, Chicago: own publication, 1928.

[23] Marks, Robert W., *The Dymaxion World of Buckminster Fuller*, New York: Reinhold, 1960, pp. 24 and 25.

[24] Fuller, Richard Buckminster, *Nine Chains to the Moon*, Philadelphia/New York/London/Toronto: J. B. Lippincott Company, 1938, p. 42.

[25] See Esguevillas, Daniel, *La casa californiana. Experiencias domésticas de posguerra*, Buenos Aires: Nobuko, 2014, pp. 68-72.

[26] See Bergdoll, Barry and Christensen, Peter, *Home Delivery: Fabricating the Modern Dwelling* (exhibition catalogue), New York: The Museum of Modern Art, 2008, p. 21.

[27] Lavalou, Armelle (ed.), *Jean Prouvé par lui-même*, Paris: Éditions du Linteau, 2001.

[28] Lapuerta, José María de, "*Prefabrication and Housing: Light Alternatives*", *AV Monografías*, 149 (*Jean Prouvé 1901-1984*), Madrid, May-June 2011, p. 83.

[29] See Gropius, Walter, "Flach-, Mittel- oder Hochbau?", in *Rationelle Bebauungsweisen*, Frankfurt: Englert & Schlosser, 1931.

[30] Le Corbusier, *La Charte d'Athènes*, Paris: Éditions de Minuit, 1957.

Wellbeing

The potential benefits of modernity were heralded at the start of the twentieth century. However, the promises of the Fordist logic ultimately fell short and, moreover, the advantages were by no means enjoyed by all. As a result, and in the wake of several economic crises and two World Wars, alternative proposals focused not on a search for greater universal (and unaffordable) progress, but rather for personal wellbeing. Instead of resorting to large, all-encompassing projects that would solve everything for an ideal society, interest shifted to small, tailor-made initiatives.

The advantages of the modern home seemed to be the exclusive domain of a small number of brilliant architects, extraordinary clients, experimental schemes and unique political moments. As a result, there was a widespread view that the modernist approach was just empty talk. In many cases, technological progress had become mere aesthetic; houses needed to cater not only for functionality, but also for personal interests and dreams. Le Corbusier had championed the home for the "ordinary man", but he also warned: "Dwelling is not only about eating, sleeping, etc., but also about having a place to think."[1]

Constructing mass-produced, adaptable and industrialised housing is a difficult endeavour; no wonder, then, that even Le Corbusier moved away from an efficiency-based approach to focus, instead, on the design of more introspective houses. Given this context, the CIAM V — held in Paris in 1937 under the theme "Housing and Leisure" — focused on the need to create coherent and harmonious societies.

This chapter looks at projects that redefined the meaning of "utility" as something subjective and unquantifiable. We shall see how the definition of wellbeing, in this period, focused on personal comfort and an interest in emotions and variability, in an attempt to build houses that could make their inhabitants happy. The first section is about homes that fostered a new concept of individuality, venturing away from the conventional idea of the family. The second one focuses on the design of pleasurable lives, in order to control the future, and the third section analyses the post-war "American Dream" home. The fourth section brings together several critiques of the cumbersome houses that were built under the misconceptions of modernity, and the final section features examples of individual shelters built as personal explorations or manifestos for unique lives.

A Room of One's Own

"To those who, absorbed with the problem of the machine for living, claimed 'architecture means service', we answered, 'architecture means emotions'."

Le Corbusier

The unitary image of modern architecture was undermined by events that challenged the established models, from the economic crisis of 1929 to the women's emancipation movements and the discovery of the realm of subconscious psychology based on Sigmund Freud's theories. These circumstances gave rise to various responses from individuals not among the closed circle of European and American architects — that is to say, architects and designers who were not invited to the International Congresses of Modern Architecture (CIAM), who were not included at the legendary 1932 exhibition *International Style* at New York's Museum of Modern Art MoMA), or who were included but sought to offer alternatives to the functionalist orthodoxy of the day. Speaking in 1929 as the host of CIAM II, Ernst May questioned the effectiveness of the architect amid the ongoing the housing crisis: "How many failures would have been avoided if every architect of a small house had been obliged to live with a working family for a couple of weeks before starting to design and build?"[2]

Ernst May had spelt out the problem: the issue of housing required a deeper, more human understanding, along with a different role for women inside and outside of the home. In *A Room of One's Own* (1929),[3] Virginia Woolf denounced the oppressive quality of houses that lacked space for individuality, and, in turn, she called into question the supposed advances of modern architecture. The real-life benefits of rationalising spaces, on the basis of efficiency charts, were few and far between; the room could in fact be a place for memory, identity and intimacy, as Woolf had argued.

Wellbeing

By looking into what had been left out of the standardised "moulds" for modern living, a broader understanding of the issues around housing began to emerge. For example, the Pan American Congress of Architects, which began eight years before the first CIAM, highlighted the unique qualities of different territories and traditions, as well as the differences between rural and urban housing. They also addressed the complexities that were omitted from the logics of mass production and the "grid city" designed from scratch. After all, cities already existed, so they had to be dealt with, along with their inhabitants.

Exhibitions were the ideal forum for imagining alternative living arrangements for the kinds of users who did not fit into the standardised moulds. Three housing prototypes, designed for exhibitions in the 1920s and 1930s, illustrate this search for new forms of habitation: an apartment designed by Charlotte Perriand, for the *L'Equipement de l'habitation* exhibition at the Salon d'Automne in Paris (1929), and two houses by Mies van der Rohe [fig. 26] and Lilly Reich for the *Die Wohnung unserer Zeit* [The Dwelling of Our Time] exposition in Berlin (1931). The designers of these three projects ignored the pre-established concepts of the bedroom and the traditional family: they aimed to rethink the relationship between furniture, activities and living space, with an emphasis on individuality, the "room of one's own" that Woolf demanded.

Charlotte Perriand created her show apartment in collaboration with Le Corbusier and Pierre Jeanneret. A couple of years beforehand, she had turned her own apartment (where she lived with her new husband) into a radically modern interior, experimenting with chrome and glass furniture. She presented these ideas in a 1927 exhibition at the Salon des Artistes Décorateurs, which took a broader perspective on the needs of a house's different inhabitants. Perriand took this vision even further in her 1929 apartment, which was a place for dynamic, temporary living, inspired by the travel trunk. These ideas were not unconnected from her personal experiences: at the time, Perriand was about to split up with her husband and move to another

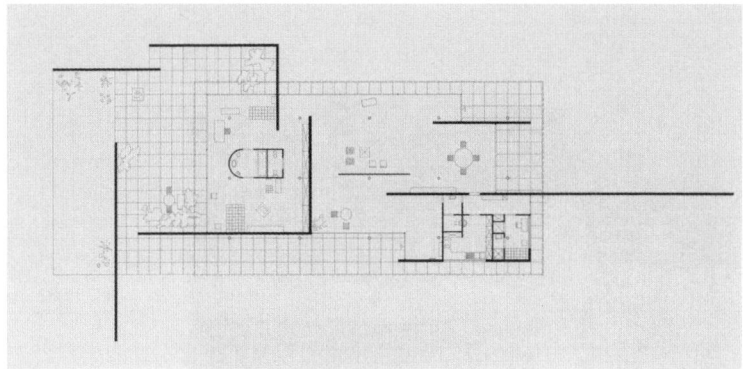

26

house. So, the removable shelves and changeable components echoed the fleeting circumstances and unexpected events in life. Perriand thought of the industrialised home as a transformable, personal item, with a moveable bed, an extendable table and metal shelves that could be arranged in different ways. Her designs revolutionised not only the concept of furniture, but also the unfixed relationships between objects, people and spaces.

The two prototype non-family homes built by Mies van der Rohe and Lilly Reich for the 1931 exhibition in Berlin — where Mies was director and Reich artistic director — reflect the search for new forms of living. Inside the huge exhibition hall, they built two full-scale models, designed with childless couples or single people in mind: these homes would offer spatial flexibility, economical solutions and lightweight furniture to cater to the different lifestyles that were emerging in society. Furthermore, these models blurred the inside-outside division. The two houses were linked by a wall and connected via a courtyard, and in both cases the bedrooms were designed so that couples could have separate spaces. Not surprisingly, these new models were proposed by two people who had rejected marriage and family life, and their personal and working relationship defied the established norms. In this exhibition,

27

Reich also designed two apartments for the Boarding-Haus, again intended for singles or couples without children. Conceptually, her approach to the Boarding-Haus was similar to that of the first interior she made, the Women's House (Haus der Frau) in Cologne's Deutscher Werkbund in 1914. The Women's House was designed to reduce the time spent by women on housework, and help them achieve independence. In these projects by Reich, as well as those of Perriand, the walls were no longer elements that enclosed the inhabitants: their work made architecture shift from the efficient to the pleasurable.

In a different cultural context, that of Mexico City, two houses demonstrate the new focus on the particularities of different bodies and activities: the studio-house for painters Diego Rivera and Frida Kahlo (Altavista, 1932) [fig. 27], designed by Juan O'Gorman, and the Blue House in Coyoacán, where Frida was born and died. Diego and Frida lived in both, but the differences between the two houses demonstrate how their vision evolved towards a more complex idea of wellbeing. The Altavista house consisted of three independent cells: a studio-house each for Diego and Frida, and a photographic studio for Frida's father. This layout dispensed with the usual division between spaces for living, socialising and working: it was a manifesto that addresses issues of individuality and independence. O'Gorman did away with the forced coexistence between the inhabitants, and also between the inhabitants and the domestic service. He detached the house from the burden of history and that of the conventional family roles. Two years after they moved into the house, Frida left Diego and moved back to her childhood home in Coyoacán. When the couple reunited, they lived there together in the late 1930s. The Coyoacán house changed over time, especially when Diego bought the adjacent lot and built an annex in collaboration with O'Gorman. Frida preferred living in the Coyoacán house, not only for the sake of comfort (it was on a single floor, which saved her the trouble of going up and down the stairs; she had reduced mobility due to her physical impediments), but also because she had made it her own. While the architect of the Altavista house had predetermined every aspect of it, the Coyoacán house was the result of improvised adaptations, based on its users' particular needs. Frida turned the room where she was born into her studio, the house had several guests over the years, and everything revolved around the coexistence between the different activities, people and context. While the Altavista house was a modern functionalist model, the Coyoacán house was an adaptation of an historic house that reflected a taste for craftsmanship, full of nooks and crannies.

A drawing of the Coyoacán house by Frida illustrates the varied relations between spaces, uses, belongings and dreams. A seemingly irrelevant part of it, like the outdoor space for drying clothes, becomes a realm full of personal meanings — it is not something to be erased by the image of a sterile modernity. The house as a realm of intimacy, in tune with memories, was not defined by the architecture, but rather by experiences. It is not surprising, therefore, that although O'Gorman championed the reproducibility of the house from a functionalist perspective — he was the first Latin American architect to build a radically modern house — when he built his own home towards the end of his life, his vision had changed completely: this time, he was guided by a profound, personal search and a deep understanding of the place. This house in San Jerónimo was one of his last projects, and the only one in which he believed he had truly produced architecture. He sculpted this home in a lava cave in El Pedregal, shaping a unique element with his own hands: he managed to bring together landscape, house and the history of the place.

Personal Paradises for the Future

"The house must act as a generator for the individual."

Frederick Kiesler

After the end of World War II (1939-45), the desire for a fresh start for humanity led to the concept of houses as controlled bubbles in which personal wellbeing could be pursued. Since universal progress was impossible, the aim was at least to create pleasurable micro-worlds. Two prototype homes represent the values sought in these new post-industrial interior realms, centred on the body and physical sensations: Frederick Kiesler's Endless House and Alison and Peter Smithson's House of the Future. Although these two futuristic caves were solely for exhibitions, they both reflect a shift in the concepts that defined the house.

Kiesler spent decades working on the Endless House [fig. 28], which he first devised in 1947. It consisted of undulating concrete caverns, a synthesis of painting, sculpture, scenography and architecture, with an air of Dadaism and Surrealism. His idea was to produce an elastic space: the house as a living creature. The name of the project not only refers to the shape of the house but also the process; his concept initially appeared in manifesto form, first in "La Cité en l'air" (1926),[4] which criticised the construction of "coffin houses", and later in "Manifeste du Corréalisme" (1949),[5] which called for inhabitants to get involved with the factors that determined the physical, psychic and social aspects of their lives. He wanted this to be reflected in a new style of home and living, with a holistic concept of the body that dispensed with the divisions between rationality and dreams. This project was a critique to the "industrial dictatorship" of machine houses: "Machine-age houses are divisions of cubicles. One box next to another. One

28

box below another. One box above another."[6] His remedy was a spatial continuity, designed for relaxation, sex and harmony with nature.

The Smithsons' House of the Future (London, 1956) [fig. 29] created a world that aimed to improve people's wellbeing by means of industrial design. It was built for the *Daily Mail Ideal Home* exhibition, which set out to show what life would be like in 25 years' time. The Smithsons' proposal even included its future inhabitants: at the exhibition, the house was occupied by actor-residents whose postures, attire, furniture and household goods combined to create a total environment, arranged around a courtyard. Here, the home became something disposable, playful, sexy, in a sensualisation of the domestic space influenced by Surrealism, Expressionism and Pop Art: the house was turned into a consumer object, in the context of a new mass culture interested in textures, colour, air conditioning, technology and the introduction (into the domestic sphere) of new materials like resin and fibreglass. The Smithsons intend-

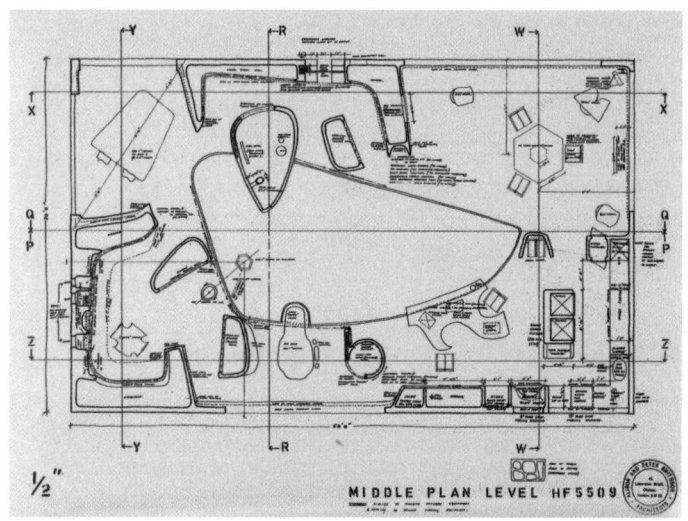

29

ed the house to be built in reinforced plastic, but due to time constraints — it had to be built in ten days — it ended up being a simulation, a kind of shop window for an ideal life, which Peter defined not as housing, but as theatre.[7]

Kiesler's Endless House and the Smithsons' House of the Future were continuous surfaces: the floors, ceilings and walls formed a single skin. However, they also had further similarities, beyond their spatial fluidity, as both houses followed an intuitive approach and were proponents of formless architecture. Unlike other houses being built at the time, these ones were based on the idea of subtraction, rather than construction: they were carved objects, and their interiors were more than just the mere gap between the modular structure and its outer envelope (as was the skin-and-bones vision of the modern canon). This architecture — somewhere between a laboratory of the future and an ancient cave — was not supposed to be "simple", in order to respond to deeper issues: complex houses for complex lives. The two projects differed, however, in an aspect that evidenced the shift towards a new era: the Endless House was based on the senses, while the House of the Future — designed for an exhibition aimed at selling the latest household products — was geared towards the emerging consumer society. In this sense, the Smithsons proposed a rupture with the outside in a new concept of privacy: contact with the world was only possible via new technology, such as the television, telephone and radio.

Arne Jacobsen and Flemming Lassen also designed a House of the Future for an exhibition (in 1929), and it can be considered a distant forerunner of the Smithsons' proposal. This house — cylindrical in shape, and laid out around a central atrium — was a device to connect the latest technology: an extension to park a car, another one for a motorboat and a heliport on the rooftop. Similarly, the Smithsons' House of the Future also revolved around a central courtyard, but it lacked façades and an external image: it was a membrane whose only point of contact with the outside was its small, controlled courtyard. At a time when air conditioning was becoming popularised in the United States and the house was being reconceived as a total, pristine shelter following the nuclear strikes on Hiroshima and Nagasaki, the Smithsons' house reflected a disconnect — both visual and physical — from the city. It was a plastic cave for a couple with no past references, without a place for children and without a city for a future life.

A few months after the Smithsons' house, another project, the Monsanto House of the Future (MHOF), was designed by Richard Hamilton and Marvin Goody, faculty members of the Massachusetts Institute of Technology. The MHOF would feature at the Future section of the recently opened Disneyland in California: it was thus right at the epicentre of a totally new form of entertainment, a disposable house for a budding consumer market promoting new forms of technology-based pleasure. There was one key difference between the MHOF and the Smithsons' House of the Future: while sales were the priority for the MHOF house, built in a country on the crest of a financial boom, the Smithsons' project represented a critical attitude to this consumerist transformation.

Designing houses of the future meant proposing new relationships between spaces and activities. Furthermore, the city and the concept of the family had to be set to one side, diluted among the new definitions of the individual and their body. These houses came from people's desire to build a paradise of their own, and they were understood almost like a skin: these were autonomous houses for autonomous lives, even if they were fictional.

Designed Lives

"If you want to change a man, change his apartment."

Paul B. Preciado

After World War II, the victorious return of American soldiers caused a boom in the housing market and that of its by-products, in line with a new ideal based on prosperity. The US population grew by 40% between 1946 and 1964 — 76.4 million baby boomers — and the country's production doubled, with an increase in house-building that reflected a concept of well-being based on leisure, consumption and the domestic redeployment of war technology. The post-war "American Dream" homes, described as houses for better living, were surrounded by gardens, and relied on appliances and cars. They were idealised environments, in a mixture of nostalgic country life and new technology-based comfort. The house thus ceased to be a machine for living, and became the symbol of a life of abundance. In the first post-war decade in the United States, the number of cars quadrupled each year, two-thirds of the population bought a television set, and, in just two years, home air-conditioning businesses grew by 500%.[8] All this happened while basic products were still being rationed in many European cities.

California became the stage for optimistic lifestyles based on Hollywood movie models and the domestic family life yearned-for during the war years. A new kind of house emerged in this context, under the influence of the country's pragmatic tradition and the avant-garde spirit imported by exiled European architects like Rudolph M. Schindler, Richard Neutra, Ludwig Mies van der Rohe, Walter Gropius and Marcel Breuer, to name but a few. Buckminster Fuller's Dymaxion House was one example of the local pragmatic tradition, while the avant-garde influence could be seen in Schindler's Schindler-Chace House. These examples, discussed in previous chapters, reflect two almost antagonistic trends that led to the emergence of the post-war house: the first one was based on the use of technology to create controlled environments, and the second one was built with traditional materials and opened to the exterior in order to enjoy the pleasant Californian climate. The former heralded technical supremacy in the form of prefab buildings and futuristic devices — pneumatic swing doors, recycled water and air purification systems — while the latter used timber in a reinterpretation of vernacular architecture, in keeping with a laidback lifestyle. These two extremes came together in a new domesticity that promised instant gratification, a far cry from the austerity of Europe's modern architecture.

In that period, design became a key element for improving the quality of life: it was about "better living through better design",[9] by bringing together new technology and the mass media. Magazines, films and exhibitions helped disseminate this architecture all around the world, with two platforms in particular playing a major role in shaping the new domestic paradigm of wellbeing: *Arts & Architecture*, a California-based magazine edited by John Entenza, and the Museum of Modern Art (MoMA) in New York. *Arts & Architecture* funded a programme devised by Entenza, the Case Study Houses, which proposed industrialised prototype houses sponsored by consumer goods companies, while the MoMA was a showcase for new trends. Both platforms encouraged experimentation, and presented the public with new possibilities.

The Case Study Houses programme was launched in the final months of World War II. An advertisement on the first few pages of the magazine sums up the spirit of the time: a typical suburban house is about to be demolished by a huge axe, with a sign above it that reads "Chop away the undesirable".[10] The ad not only referred to the need to build millions of new houses, but also to remodel existing ones. At the time, 33% of American families — roughly fifty million people — were inadequately housed, which meant that a large part of the population would either demand new houses or need to renovate their old ones.[11] The magazine canvassed for new model homes in its Case Study Houses programme, and presented a catalogue of available suppliers. Between 1945 and 1967, twenty-six Case Study Houses were built by leading California-based designers including Eero Saarinen, Charles and Ray Eames, Richard Neutra, Pierre Koenig and Craig Ellwood. These houses, transformed into an advertising campaign, were physically and conceptually close to the Hollywood movie industry. Case Study House No. 8 (1949) [fig. 30] is a good example of the programme's success. It was built by Charles and Ray Eames for themselves, to showcase the on-site assembly of mail-order components. While they waited for the off-the-shelf parts to be available, they decided to modify the project and use the prefabricated elements in a different way. The house was assembled in less than two days and showed off the variability of the system. This was even more evident when comparing the house to the one built by Charles Eames and Saarinen for Entenza on the adjacent lot, with the same materials as the previous one, but resolved in a completely different way.

In the early 1940s, the MoMA exhibited fully furnished prototype houses by Fuller, Breuer, and Gregory Ain in its sculpture garden. The new role of the post-war house was made explicit in the press release for Fuller's portable prototype, the Dymaxion Deployment Unit, renamed the Defense House when it was erected at the MoMA in 1941: "A Shelter in War — A Beach House in Peacetime". The headline of one newspaper critique, "How to be Comfortable Though Bombed",[12] reflects the priorities at the time: relaxing, sturdy homes, despite what might be happening outside. This model not only encouraged the house's independence from its urban, political and natural surroundings, but also the autonomy of its inhabitants. The house thus became an element for both protection and personal enjoyment, as well as a display item that made the intimacy of the domestic space publicly visible.

30

A few years later, Elizabeth Bauer Mock curated an exhibition at the MoMA titled *Tomorrow's Small House* (1945). It included houses designed by a dozen renowned architects, such as Frank Lloyd Wright and Philip Johnson, and it served as a prelude to the transition from war to peacetime in terms of housing. The exhibition was a warning to the country that it would need to build more than a million houses a year when the war was over, so it was a way to encourage people to think about new forms of living; the models showed an indissoluble link between design and quality of life.[13] In the exhibition catalogue, Bauer Mock defined the new key concepts in housing: prefabrication, variety, open floor plan, economy, visual spaciousness by means of glass façades and a connection with the surroundings. The models, spot-lit against the black backdrop of the exhibition rooms, were placed at eye level, literally opening up the houses to viewers. *Tomorrow's Small House* seemed to broadcast a subliminal message about the future: following a period of decline in the cities, a new light was emerging via these houses on public display.

The Case Study Houses and MoMA promoted the idea of houses placed in abstract sites (as exhibition items), based on the triad of form, style and technology. These houses were more visited and published than actually lived in, and they were by no means economical: they became luxury objects for the cultural elite. In most cases, the construction methods were not industrialised, and specialised labour was needed to assemble them. Unsurprisingly, they received all kinds of criticism, including the question asked by Neutra's staff on tackling new projects: "What will be the best material to use for the next steel house?"[14] A lot had changed in a short time. In 1943, two years before launching the Case Study Houses programme, John Entenza put a call out for the design of a 100 m^2 house that would be a manifesto for affordable prefabrication. In 1962, nearly 20 years later, when Entenza left his editor's post at *Arts & Architecture*, the Case Study Houses were three times that size, with double-height spaces and swimming pools. This transition from the minimal to the luxury house not only reflects the evolution from proposals born in Europe under the *Existenzminimum* precepts to the fantasy architecture of Hollywood or Disneyland, but it also illustrates the transformation of the domestic environment into an exhibition object, in which image prevailed over accessibility: it didn't seem to matter whether the proposals were affordable for the entire population, or for just a few.

These show homes for a new global culture camouflaged an alarming reality, i.e. the rise of vast housing developments. A particularly striking example was Levittown, Pennsylvania, where more than 17,000 single-family dwellings were constructed in just six years (an entire house could be built in just one day). By 1965, some 65,000 people were living in Levittown's repetitive street blocks, a way of life far removed from the dream of individuality heralded at the time in speeches

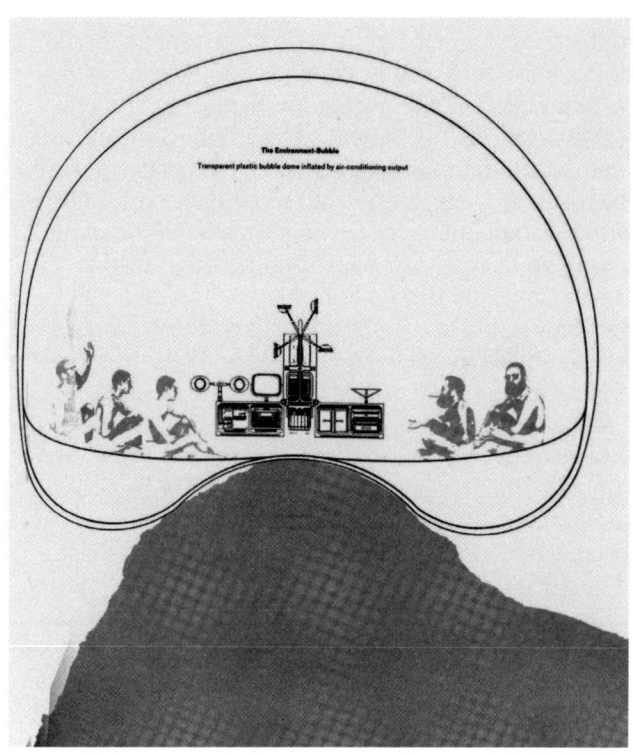

31

about the superiority of American democracy. The Levittown model spread across the country, and it soon became the nightmare of suburbia. In that same year, 1965, a number of race riots broke out in Los Angeles, marking the end of the American Dream and the start of the urban crisis of the post-modern metropolis.

1965 also saw the publication of Reyner Banham's essay "A Home Is Not a House",[15] in which he set out the need to redefine the limits to the mechanisation of housebuilding. He also criticised the environmental impact of the American model of energy-intensive, isolated, single-family dwellings. Banham focused on the crisis caused by the excessive dependence between houses and technology, which segregated society and harmed the planet. His essay was accompanied by François Dallegret's drawings [fig. 31], in which the anatomy of a house is shown as a bundle of pipes, and the house itself was a polyethylene bubble to store food, energy and a television set. Banham came up with the concept of the *unhouse*, a shell defined by its installations — an icon of the new pop culture and the re-creation of seemingly perfect environments — as well as the *anti-city*, referring to life in the suburbs, a perfect example of which was the endless sprawl of Los Angeles. The motto for the preceding decades seemed to have been, "plant houses, not potatoes", and it led Americans, 6% of the world's population, to consume one third of the planet's non-renewable resources, and own almost half of the world's cars (with more cars than children per family).[16]

The everyday reality was completely different to the idealised image of modernity: household appliances did not reduce household chores, although they did raise hygiene standards and led to the production of more sophisticated food. The size of houses grew constantly, as did the number of products that increased the time and money spent on the home. This model — the house as an autonomous cell to be filled with novel products — spread around the world, as did its inconsistencies. One problem was the fact that Americans had the largest amount of private residential space per person in all human history, with 30% of their homes containing seven or more rooms. However, 35% of all houses were inhabited by just one person, and 50% of families did not live with their offspring.[17] The unsustainable effects of suburban houses soon rocketed: these houses were located far away from the workplace, they consumed huge amounts of energy and were unaffordable for most people. Banham followed up "A Home Is Not a House" with *The Architecture of the Well-tempered Environment* (1969),[18] in which he elaborated on the environmental impact of constructions and the limits to the concept of wellbeing that depended on technical services. He also addressed fundamental architectural issues, as part of a broader view of the relationship between the environment, technology and habitability, whereby individual satisfaction ought to be compatible with collective wellbeing.

The Ridicule of the Modern House

"I have never seen what is usually considered to be an architect-designed home that was not a monstrosity."

John Burroughs

In the mid-twentieth century, people began to question the supposed advantages of modernity and reject the super-aestheticisation of life. Houses were parodied in movies and literature as a way to critique people's obsession with technological inventions that seemed like science fiction, but were in fact becoming part of everyday life. *How to Live in a Flat* (1936),[19] by W. Heath Robinson and K. R. G. Browne [fig. 32], caricatured the effects of human coexistence in vertical apartment blocks, which had heralded great benefits, yet drawn widespread scepticism. The book included drawings that mocked apartment life, in cities taken over by towers of clotheslines. It also depicts new drawbacks, such as high windows that were impossible to clean, walls so thin that they bent, and the complete lack of privacy from neighbours, who literally live right on top. In the 1930s, parodies like this spoke of an incipient future, but by the 1950s it had almost become a reality: there were tables that changed shape at the push of a button, plastic houses and robotic vacuum cleaners. The house had become a self-enclosed, disposable entity, connected to the outside world via technology: the television, radio, telephone and car were now indispensable parts of the home. This was a time when housework was encouraged not as work, but as an enjoyable and fun activity. In fact, the recasting of the house as a playground of gadgets was a front: domestic functionality had been warped into a new kind of slavery.

These controversies were anticipated by Buster Keaton and Eddie Cline in two short films, *One Week* (1920) and *The Electric*

32

Economical arrangement of bedroom space in a converted house

House (1922), which warn of the problems ensuing from naive trust in the modern house. In both cases, human errors make dreams of prosperity turn into a nightmare. In the first film, *One Week*, a newlywed couple try to assemble their house from a kit of prefab components. Unwittingly, they follow an altered set of instructions, and end up assembling a botched house with the front door on the top floor, the balcony on the ground floor and the roof upside down. The house can't withstand the force of the wind, and it is blown onto a railway line, where a passing train runs into it and destroys it. This film derided the blind repetition of housing models, and illustrated the gulf between inhabitants' desires, their needs and the built reality. In *The Electric House*, modifications to the electrical wiring in a house also trigger a chain of disasters. A number of modern inventions — an escalator, an automatic dumbwaiter, a folding bed and a mobile bathtub — begin to rebel against their users, throwing plates at their faces and crushing them. In both films, the underlying theme was the loss of the home — houses that turn against their inhabitants — and the fragility of the human being overwhelmed by new technology, uncomfortable furniture and dubious inventions that disturbed the normal daily life. As with the illustrations in *How to Live in a Flat*, they showed a clash between brand-new new technology (lifts, metal structures and huge windows) and the traditional clothes of the time (top hats, gloves and corsets), in an image which in fact differed little from the attire of architects Mies van der Rohe and Le Corbusier when they met at the Weissenhofsiedlung in Stuttgart, photographed beside their innovative houses wearing bowler hats, bow ties and opera pumps.

The house, like no other typology, was the setting for the mismatch between old traditions and new inventions. During this era, there were growing concerns not only about the impact of new appliances like refrigerators and electric irons, which were already in widespread use by the 1950s, but also about the unprecedented changes to cities and families as a result of the transformations brought about by women's emancipation, women's work outside the home and urban sprawl.

If You Want to Build a House,[20] a 1936 exhibition at MoMA, curated by Elizabeth Bauer Mock, is a good example of the mismatch between the attractive modern house and its potential flaws. The images in the exhibition catalogue highlight the contrasts: photographs of attractive houses built by pioneers of modern architecture (such as Frank Lloyd Wright, Walter Gropius and Philip Johnson) sit alongside drawings by cartoonist Robert C. Osborn that illustrate the fears people had about modernity being brought into their everyday lives. Photographs of bright spaces, looking over the landscape, share pages with comical depictions of glass fishbowls and claustrophobic faces in dark caverns. *If You Want to Build a House* encapsulated and disseminated the theoretical debates of the day, just as the curator's sister Catherine K. Bauer had done in her famous book, *Modern Housing* (1934).[21] The Bauer sisters' work discussed the pros and cons of the modern house, and summarised the core dilemmas in the search for a balance between genuine innovation and the caricatured image of modernity.

Two of Jacques Tati's films, *Mon Oncle* (1958) and *Playtime* (1967), also question the priorities of modernised lifestyles. *Mon Oncle* mocks the mechanised house, enviable in appearance but uncomfortable for its inhabitants, while *Playtime* is a critique of modernity in newly urbanised settings. *Mon Oncle* mocks the absurdity of "progress" in the modern house, designed for a model family that only has a place in statistics. Nine years later, *Playtime* took the principles of the modern movement to an extreme, showing the effects of industrialisation on an impersonal city characterised by urban problems and social breakdown.

Interestingly, both of these films reflect the issues debated at the CIAMs in the 1940s and 50s: that is, post-war urban reconstruction and how to deal with the problems of segregation that modernity had brought about.[22] From CIAM VI (Bridgewater, 1947) to CIAM XI (Otterlo, 1959), the central theme of "urban reidentification" aimed to reestablish a more human condition, and encourage greater harmony between the individual sphere and collective wellbeing.

At the last CIAMs, internal conflicts grew between the "old guard" and the younger members: the latter were dissatisfied with the reductionist vision that overlooked the complex nature of human realities.[23] After CIAM IX, held in Aix-en-Provence in 1953, *The Habitat Charter* was drafted to replace *The Athens Charter*,[24] due to pressure from a group of young people led by Alison and Peter Smithson, Aldo van Eyck and Giancarlo De Carlo, among others, who founded Team X as a rejection of the principles of the pre-war CIAMs.[25] Influenced by new empiricism or "new humanism", Team X sought to address human complexity, place a greater emphasis on symbolism, and repair the broken relations caused by pseudo-functionalist subdivision. The following year, 1954, Team X drew up a manifesto, "Statement on Habitat", later retitled the "Doorn Manifesto", which called for a more comprehensive understanding of the relationships between housing, topography, climate and traditions. Team X were opposed to the division of cities into four segments — housing, transportation, work and leisure — and they instead proposed four interconnections based on different scales and more natural ways of grouping people: house, street, district and city. Team X claimed that the destruction of the city was not only due to the war, but also because of the ineptitude of architects and urban planners, who had become used to applying the rigid principles of *The Athens Charter*: as Team X saw it, the prevalent architects had essentially been acting like the protagonist of *One Week*, who put up his house by following assembly instructions that turned out to be wrong.

The problems of this period were summed up by Ernesto Nathan Rogers, editor of *Domus* magazine: "On every side the house of man is fissured (if it were a boat, we should say it leaks). We should hurry to it with some bricks, or beams, or sheets of glass and, instead of it, here we are with a Magazine. We give no bread to the hungry, no raft to the ship-wrecked, only words."[26] This critique marked the end of three decades that had been steered by the principles of the modern movement, in which houses were planned for ideal inhabitants and universal-yet-incompatible lives. The demise of the CIAMs was announced at the tenth Congress in 1956, held in Dubrovnik and geared towards "Habitat, the problem of relationships". The final CIAM was held at Otterlo in 1959, with the desire to forge new paths towards less potentially risible architectures.

Empire Cabins

"At a certain age, most children feel the urge to build some kind of shelter."

Steen Eiler Rasmussen

The world's population grew exponentially in the mid-twentieth century, as did the size of cities. This development prompted a search for new, harmonious relationships between the individual, architecture and nature. Four shelters/cabins built between the 1940s and 60s as personal explorations by their inhabitants — Ralph Erskine, Le Corbusier, Jean Prouvé and Richard Buckminster Fuller — redefined the meaning of wellbeing, not on the basis of canons but on the basis of their actual use.

These four shelters were reminiscent of similar cabin/manifestos built in the mid-nineteenth and early twentieth centuries by Henry D. Thoreau, Gustav Mahler, Ludwig Wittgenstein and Martin Heidegger, all of whom had called for congruence between ways of living and the environment. Thoreau spent two years living in a 14 m² cabin he built for himself near the shore of Walden Pond, where he envisioned a self-sufficient lifestyle and — way ahead of his time — questioned the sense of having a house if there is no sustainable planet on which to place it. The experience inspired his most famous book, *Walden* (1854),[27] a treatise in defence of a life based on the essentials. As for Mahler, he built three cabins in different locations, driven by a similar search for an alternative to houses that did not align with his inner world. He lived in the first two as a bachelor, and shared the last one with his wife, but they all repeated the same layout of a single space, the area he needed to move around his piano. Wittgenstein built a minimal cell on a Norwegian fjord, where he spent long periods in isolation over almost four decades, writing and trying to comprehend the purest state of human existence. Heidegger also lived intermittently for fifty years in a 6 × 7-metre hut that he built in the Black Forest, Germany, where he wrote some of his most important texts. Heidegger attributed the housing problem not to the lack of houses, but to the alienation of the human being from the essence of habitation. He felt that his hut brought him closer to a more complete and honest existence, one that was absorbed in the environment. When his wife and children lived with him during the holidays, he even rented a room in a nearby house to maintain the isolation he desired.

These four cabins were manifestos of the house as an intimate refuge and a place for authenticity. However, it is important to remember that they were temporary abodes, an existentialist myth where the core elements of the habitat were nature, memory and place.

On the other hand, Erskine, Le Corbusier, Prouvé and Fuller built their own modest shelters as laboratories where they could self-test their theories about inhabiting, in a spirit halfway between craftsmanship and engineering. Although they shared their forerunners' preference for wood, for the economical use of resources and a sense of isolation, these newer constructions differed in one fundamental aspect: they were no longer built in the image of the primitive hut mythologised by Abbot Marc-Antoine Laugier centuries beforehand. Instead, they were reinterpretations based on a new relationship between technology, materials and place. The user was no longer an essentialist romantic but rather a tireless designer, convinced that the lessons of the past could be used to inspire innovation. Respecting the land now meant devising new building systems, and reducing architecture to its core purpose did not mean doing as little as possible: it was about rethinking every single part, in defiance of a world that was lacking experimental efforts and places that were truly one's own. These architects wanted to perfect the basic housing unit, and although for many years these projects were considered minor works in their careers, they were opportunities for them to rethink their stance amid a personal quest for wellbeing.

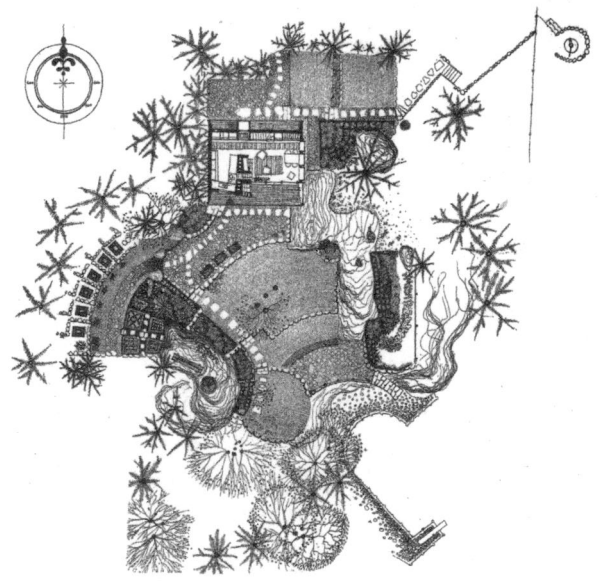

33

Erskine built The Box on the outskirts of Stockholm (Lådan, 1942) [fig. 33] with his own hands, helped by his wife Ruth. Although it was a minimal room, 22 m² and 2.1 m high, built from materials found on site, it was his family home and workplace for nearly four years, during which time he made adaptations to improve its thermal insulation and respond to new needs. In plan, Erskine's design covered an area twelve times larger than the built footprint because the outdoor zones were part of the house too. Several mobile elements shaped a multi-purpose space: a bed was hung from the ceiling and raised with ropes and pulleys to free the space during the day, or else folded up to serve as a living room sofa. Also, a folding desk turned the house into an office.

In the same year that the Unité d'Habitation was officially opened in Marseilles, Le Corbusier designed Le Cabanon (Roquebrune-Cap-Martin, 1952) [fig. 34], a cottage where he

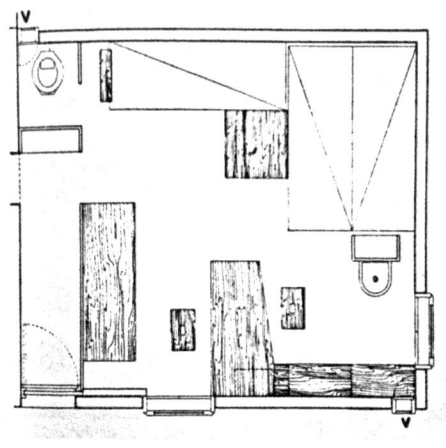

34

lived on-and-off for the last fifteen years of his life. Le Corbusier was familiar with this part of the Côte d'Azur, having spent several periods in Eileen Gray's E-1027 house. Therefore, it is not surprising that, some decades later, he built Le Cabanon on a nearby plot, inspired by Gray's approach to designing spaces: that is, with an intimate connection to the furniture, the body, the activities and the place. In this shelter, measuring less than 14 m^2, Le Corbusier pushed to the limit his study of prefab domestic prototypes, which he first investigated for his Dom-Ino House. On that project, he had consulted engineer Max du Bois to help him design an industrialised house based on a concrete skeleton. For Le Cabanon, he teamed up with Jean Prouvé and carpenter Charles Barberis to build the different parts of his elaborate shelter-hut. Le Cabanon's design was based on the Modulor rule of harmony, devised by Le Corbusier, and was inspired by minimalist ship cabins and their shared facilities. The small cell was functional thanks to a nearby tavern, where he would go and eat, and a small nearby hut that he subsequently built as a separate workspace. Le Cabanon was a perfection of the monastic cell: the basic living unit had inspired him in

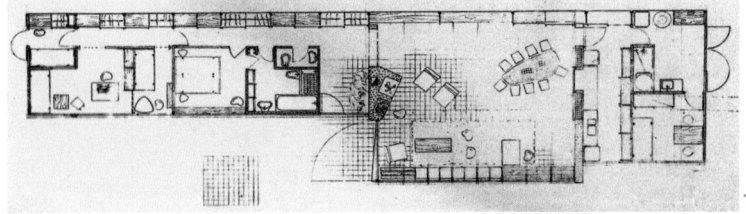
35

his youth and he championed it all his life, and this is where he spent his last days.

Prouvé built a collage-house on a steep hillside in Nancy, France. He assembled it in 1953 with the help of his family: it was made from the leftover parts of his prefab prototypes, making the most of industrial progress to achieve the highest possible quality at the lowest possible cost. Prouvé finally succeeded, not through his initial aspiration to be the Henry Ford of housing, but by adapting architecture to the site and its specific requirements. His earlier projects were prototypes for nomadic lives, but his house in Nancy [fig. 35] was his stable abode until his old age. In this project, he finally managed to combine the roles of designer and builder, as he had always desired. And there was another key aspect, i.e. that of user participation as a fundamental part of the process.

Richard Buckminster Fuller built the frame of his dome house (Illinois, 1960) [fig. 36] in just seven hours. His geodesic domes were considered the strongest and lightest way to cover a space, and he set out to prove that his invention could be turned into an affordable house. The instantaneous covering — measuring twelve metres in diameter, attached to a timber frame — weighed no more than a car.[28] His concern about the impact of housing on the planet led him to make his dome-house a self-contained microcosm that could be installed anywhere in the world. Fuller defended the idea that houses ought to be places of care and nurture, and that they should eradicate exploitation and selfishness. However, none of this was being

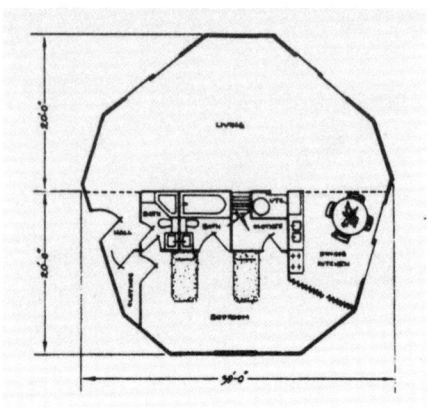

36

done by architects, whom he described as "shelter tailors". Consequently, "architects [should be] the first piece of equipment to be replaced".[29] His ambition was to produce houses that tackled fatigue and depression. Thirty years after building his prototype Dymaxion (1927), his ultralight dome-house succeeded in changing the concept of a house from a place that was protected against the world to one that made the best use of it: he went from creating bunker houses to designing floating clouds for an environmentally-aware mobile society. In 1964, Fuller appeared on the cover of *Time* magazine, his face in the shape of a geodesic dome, with a helicopter carrying another dome through the air. This heralded a new era of sci-fi scenarios that ultimately came true.

The cabins designed by Erskine, Le Corbusier, Prouvé and Fuller encouraged a similar sense of personal wellbeing to the houses built in the 1950s by Alvar Aalto on Muuratsalo Island, Alison and Peter Smithson in the Wiltshire countryside, Charles and Ray Eames in Los Angeles, Lina Bo Bardi in São Paulo [fig. 37] and Luis Barragán [fig. 38] and Juan O'Gorman [fig. 39] in Mexico City. In all these experimental homes — in which the architects themselves lived — the architect/user redefined the relations between building, memory, dreams and the landscape, in two ways. In the case of Erskine, Le Corbusier, Prouvé, Aalto, Bo Bardi, Barragán and O'Gorman, influenced by Maurice

37

38

39

Merleau-Ponty's phenomenology and existentialism, this was an introspective search for a space based on the user's experience as the creator of their own life. Meanwhile, in the USA, a second trend — exemplified by Fuller, and Charles and Ray Eames — was based on technology and visual representation, aimed at turning any object into a marketable product. The former group sought intimate

refuge, while the latter presented the house as a stage.
The main changes in this period can be seen in the transition from the influence of existentialism, based on physical experience, to the pre-eminence of the visual experience of pop art. This interest in the representational nature of architecture led to extroverted domestic spaces. Two documentaries exemplify this: one about the construction of Fuller's dome-house and another about the Eames' home, *House: After Five Years of Living* (1955). In the former, the construction process is a pleasurable activity, reminiscent of a day spent outdoors, while in the latter, the shadows and reflections on the walls are no less important than the walls themselves, and the interior space is given the same relevance as the chairs or the vase. In both films, home life is seen as an event that takes on more importance than the house itself.

Houses became toys with their insides on display, much like the Eames' Revell Toy House (1959). Rather than removing a wall to show its section (as with a normal dollhouse), the Toy House was opened up by lifting the roof off. Similarly, in this same period, films, magazines and museums began to lift off the domestic shell in a process of redefining the home as a space open to public interaction. The Eames' Toy House, along with the documentary about their home life, marked a new perspective on the confines of the home, just as the popular magazines of the day, from *Arts & Architecture* to *Playboy*, presented a public domesticity, a "striptease" of hitherto covered-up domestic spaces. Philosopher Paul B. Preciado[30] explains that this exteriorisation of the house marked the start of a post-domestic space, with blurred boundaries between public and private, work and leisure, day and night, and natural and artificial. This new type of home was anchored in communication technology, and turned residents into actors and spectators at the same time. Far removed from the idealised prototype home for the nuclear family, the individual room began to gain prominence in the 1950s thanks to Simone de Beavouir, who promoted the advantages of living in hotel rooms, and activist

Betty Friedan, who compared the lives of women in isolated suburban homes with confinement in concentration camps.[31] In this period, discourses focused on new types of houses, removed from the binomials of freedom/slavery, indoor/outdoor, male/female, urban/country, and visible/invisible. Like the new formats for coexistence that had emerged during World War II — both in soldiers' barracks and in homes left without husbands and fathers — there was a growing need for spaces that allowed for human diversity in all its complexity.

The base references were no longer solitary cabins, but rather the widely publicised houses inhabited by stars like Andy Warhol, with his famous penthouse loft in New York's Soho, or Hugh Hefner, with his Playboy mansions in Chicago and Los Angeles. Warhol's apartment (called The Factory, rather than his "house") experimented with new notions of coexistence, while the Playboy mansions and their extensions — such as Hefner's private jet, making it "the first bachelor apartment with wings"[32] — opened the door to countless ways to consume others' privacy. These spaces were regarded as marketable worlds, which represented an assault not only on the staid concept of the nuclear family and American suburbia, but also on the division of contexts that modernity had brought about in its separation of the home from the spheres of work and pleasure. Removing the roof of a dollhouse, to lay bare its private inner world, or introducing cameras in the home, thanks to Kodachrome and Polaroid technology — whereby anyone and everyone could become a snapshot photographer — triggered the theatricalisation and de-domestication of the interior. Makeshift appropriation took precedence over the restrictive family home, and the biggest change came from visualising the home as an activity, rather than an object or a place. All this seemed to fulfil the dream of Eeron Saarinen and Charles Eames, who wrote: "House, in this case means center of productive activities."[33]

Two works of architecture by Philip Johnson exemplify the contrast between the introspective cabin and the exhibitionist

40

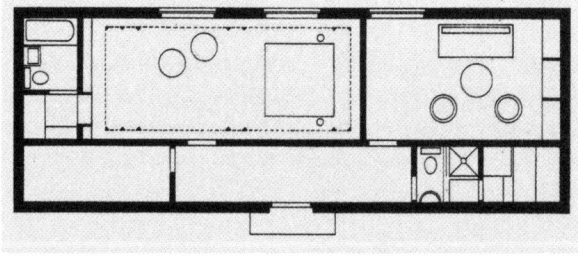

41

house: the Glass House (New Canaan, 1948) [fig. 40], and the blind volume of the Brick House (New Canaan, 1949) [fig. 41], built just a few feet apart. The former is a transparent pavilion, and the latter is an urn; both were a statement of opposition to the political and religious control over everyday life. They exemplify the search for new definitions of life that could potentially facilitate the transition from houses designed to meet basic needs to houses capable of providing amusement.

1   Llizo, Joaquín, "Unas palabras de Le Corbusier. El sutil poeta de la edificación. La emoción de lo geométrico", *El Sol*, vol. XII, 3361, Madrid, 11 May 1928, cited in Guerrero, Salvador (ed.), *Le Corbusier, Madrid 1928. Una casa-un palacio*, Madrid: Residencia de Estudiantes, 2010, p. 44.
2   Aymonino, Carlo, *L'abitazione razionale: atti dei congressi CIAM, 1929-1930*, Padua: Marsilio, 1973.
3   Woolf, Virginia, *A Room of One's Own*, London: The Hogarth Press, 1929.
4   Kiesler, Friederick, "La Cité en l'air", *G. Material zur elementaren Gestaltung*, no. 4, Berlin, March 1926.
5   Kiesler, Friederick, "Manifeste du Corréalisme", *L'Architecture d'Aujourd'hui*, no. 2, Paris, June 1949.
6   Ibid., p. 148.
7   See Colomina, Beatriz, "Friends of Future: A Conversation with Peter Smithson", *October*, 94, Cambridge (Mass.), Fall 2000.
8   See Esguevillas, Daniel, *La casa californiana. Experiencias domésticas de posguerra*, Buenos Aires: Nobuko, 2014, p. 78; and Colomina, Beatriz, *Domesticity at War*, op. cit., p. 184.
9   Eero Saarinen, quoted in Esguevillas, Daniel, op. cit., p. 44.
10 *Arts & Architecture*, no. 1, Los Angeles, January 1945, p. 4.
11 See Pawley, Martin, *Architecture versus Housing*, London: Praeger, 1971, p. 78.
12 "How to Be Comfortable Though Bombed", *The New Age Herald*, 26 October 1941; quoted in Colomina, Beatriz, *Domesticity at War*, op. cit., p. 75 and illustration on p. 117.
13 See "Tomorrow's Small House, Models and Plans", *Bulletin of The Museum of Modern Art*, vol. XII, no. 5, New York, Summer 1945, p. 4.
14 Quoted in Terrados Cepeda, Francisco Javier, *Prefabricación ligera de viviendas. Nuevas premisas*, Seville: Universidad de Sevilla, 2012, p. 30.
15 Banham, Reyner, "A Home Is Not a House", *Art in America*, no. 2, New York, April 1956, pp. 70-79.
16 See Hayden, Dolores, *Redesigning the American Dream. The Future of Housing, Work, and Family Life*, New York/London: W. W. Norton & Co., 1984, pp. 45 and 47.
17 See Hayden, Dolores, op. cit., p. 38; and Riley, Terence, *The Un-Private House*, New York: The Museum of Modern Art, 1999, p. 19.
18 Banham, Reyner, *The Architecture of the Well-tempered Environment*, London: The Architectural Press, 1969.

[19] Robinson, W. Heath and Browne, K. R. G., *How to Live in a Flat,* London: Hutchinson & Co., 1936.

[20] Bauer Mock, Elizabeth, *If You Want to Build a House* (exhibition catalogue), New York: The Museum of Modern Art, 1946.

[21] Bauer, Catherine K., *Modern Housing,* Boston/New York: Houghton Mifflin Company/The Riverside Press Cambridge, 1934.

[22] The CIAMs held after World War II were in Bridgewater (1947), Bergamo (1949), Hoddesdon (1951), Aix-en-Provence (1953), Dubrovnik (1956) and Otterlo (1959).

[23] See Bosma, Koos; Van Hoogstraten, Dorine and Vos, Martijn (eds.), *Housing for the Millions: John Habraken and the SAR (1960-2000)*, Rotterdam: NAi, 2000, pp. 53-55.

[24] Le Corbusier, *La Charte d'Athènes*, Paris: Éditions de Minuit, 1957.

[25] Team X was formed in 1954, led by Alison and Peter Smithson, Jaap Bakema, Georges Candilis, Shadrach Woods, Aldo Van Eyck, Giancarlo De Carlo and José Antonio Coderch, among others.

[26] Rogers, Ernesto Nathan, "La casa dell'uomo", *Domus*, no 205, Milan, January 1946, p. 2.

[27] Thoreau, Henry D., *Walden, or Live in the Woods*, Boston: Ticknor and Fields, 1854.

[28] See De Lózar de la Viña, Miguel, *La cabaña moderna: pequeñas arquitecturas en busca de sentido*, Buenos Aires: Diseño, 2016, p. 188.

[29] Wigley, Mark, "Broadcasting Shelter", *AV Monografías*, no. 143 (*Buckminster Fuller 1895-1983*), Madrid, May-June 2010, p. 55.

[30] See Preciado, Paul B., *Pornotopía. Arquitectura y sexualidad in 'Playboy' durante la guerra fría*, Barcelona: Anagrama, 2010 (English versión: *Pornotopia: An Essay on Playboy's Architecture and Biopolitics*, New York: Zone Books, 2014).

[31] See de Beauvoir, Simone, *Le Deuxième sexe,* Paris: Gallimard, 1949 (English version: *The Second Sex*, New York: Random House, 2011); and Friedan, Betty, *The Feminine Mystique*, London: Victor Gollancz, 1963.

[32] Preciado, Paul B., *op, cit.*

[33] *Arts & Architecture*, vol. 62, no. 12, Los Angeles, December 1945, p. 44.

Identity

Is it possible to maintain a sense of individuality in an increasingly crowded world? Is it possible to build millions of houses that match personal preferences? This chapter focuses on trends that emerged in the 1950s, 60s and 70s, the aim of which was to restore the sense of identity that industrial homogenisation had erased. In an era marked by population growth, there was a change in architecture as residents sought to regain agency over their surroundings. For example, people favoured spontaneity over standardisation, users' imagination over specialist knowledge, and being part of a community over the paralysing single-family house. New housing estates began to follow the spirit of small, local-style neighbourhoods, and houses came to be regarded as both communal and customisable universes.

The five sections in this chapter look at various types of projects in which, despite their large scale, users were able to regain control over "their" space and identify with it. The first section focuses on different types of collective housing projects with shared services, heirs to Le Corbusier's Unité d'Habitation in Marseilles. The second section addresses utopian projects that allowed the inhabitants to be the creators of adaptable worlds. The third one looks at personal instant houses, the fourth covers projects that devolved power to inhabitants as owner-builders, and the final section presents residential megastructures with a sense of individuality.

The urban planning debates of the time are analysed in Jane Jacobs' *The Death and Life of Great American Cities* (1961).[1] In this book, the author and activist called for neighbourhood collaboration as a way to counter the political and economic interests behind the large-scale urban development operations that threaten the harmony of cities, their landscape and the identity of their inhabitants. Due to the influence of anthropology and sociology, the role of architecture radically changed: this period saw the rise of community participation, and a focus on the gradients between private and communal space. The architect's task was to bring together diverse voices, and draft the guidelines — the support structures — so that users could shape their own environment. The detached, single-family house fell out of favour; customisable cells within broad communal systems were encouraged instead, with the intention of including variable desires amid a context of uncertain futures.

The City in a Building

"The ideal house is that which one can make one's own without altering anything."

Alison and Peter Smithson

In the second half of the twentieth century, there was an attempt to prove that the detached single-family house could be replaced by large housing blocks without sacrificing identity or comfort. Le Corbusier's Unité d'Habitation (Marseilles, 1952) [fig. 42] exemplifies the search for replicable dwellings with shared services and a community life, but still compatible with the development of each person's individuality. His building contained 337 apartments, in 16 different typologies, ranging from basic flats to homes for four-child families, with services, shops and a rooftop leisure space. Le Corbusier's model was repeated in thousands of other apartment blocks built in the post-war period, all around the world.

A photograph in Le Corbusier's *Complete Works*[2] shows a hand inserting a furnished dwelling into a modular structure that resembles a wine rack, similar to his vision for the Unité in Marseilles. This "social laboratory", as he described it, echoed Charles Fourier's Phalanstery and the Carthusian monastery of Ema, Tuscany, where, during a visit in his youth, Le Corbusier had noted the harmonious relationship between the privacy of the monks' cells and the monastery's community life. The photo brings to mind the picture of a transatlantic liner he had published almost two decades before in *La Ville Radieuse* (1935), which he described as "a floating apartment block".[3] The section of the transatlantic liner and the Unité d'Habitation share not only the logic of minimal spaces around common services, but also the idea of self-sufficient detached structures.

 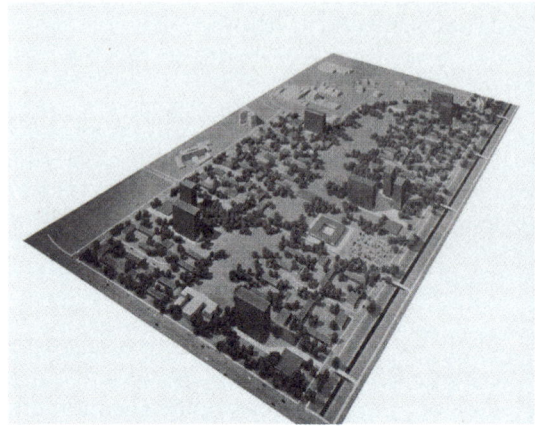

42　　　　　　　　　　43

The Unité d'Habitation in Marseilles is a synthesis of two models that describe the relationship between buildings and modern urban planning: "Towers in the Park" and "Building as Street". These two categories address the fact that cities were being taken over by cars, so they entailed residential blocks surrounded by gardens located away from the traffic — as in Le Corbusier's Contemporary City for Three Million Inhabitants (1922) — or long horizontal buildings shaped like streets, as in his projects for Rio de Janeiro (1929) and Algiers (1931). Both solutions look like something out of science fiction, but in the 1950s and 60s, they slowly began to take hold around the world. The mass production of housing, as announced years beforehand, was now coming true, leading to the proliferation of vast buildings on an unprecedented scale.

Lafayette Park (Detroit, 1963) [fig. 43] is a good example of the "Towers in the Park" model. It was designed by Mies van de Rohe, in collaboration with Ludwig Hilberseimer and landscape designer Alfred Caldwell, and combines duplex dwellings, courtyard houses and apartment blocks within a park. Lafayette gave less relevance to streets for cars, and shaped a new

44

45

kind of urban fabric based on the multiplication of the dwelling cell. Its towers do not form a concrete skyline, unlike Hilberseimer's Vertical City designed 30 years earlier, but rather they coexist with the gardens and horizontal buildings. Even so, they largely follow the same premises defended by Hilberseimer back then — differentiated routes for cars and pedestrians, modular building types and the house as the basis for a new urban development — but nature played a central role here, and gave the complex its identity.

Two Brazilian works — the Pedregulho Housing Complex by Affonso Eduardo Reidy and Carmen Portinho (Rio de Janeiro, 1952) [fig. 44], and Oscar Niemeyer's Copan Building (São Paulo, 1952) [fig. 45] — exemplify the "Building as Street" model. Pedregulho is a seven-storey waving "ribbon" that runs for 260 metres; it contains 272 dwellings, and it represented a renewed image of public housing with collective services. The building, placed on the slope of a mountain, has no lifts — thanks to its numerous paths and entrances from the hillside — and contains one-bedroom apartments and four-bedroom duplexes, all of which have good views and natural ventilation. A group of blocks at the lower part of the site, with two to four-bedroom apartments, round off a programme that also includes a school, nursery, gym, health centre, communal laundries, shops, recreational areas and gardens designed by landscape architect Roberto Burle Marx.

Niemeyer's Copan Building houses 5,000 residents in a curved, 38-storey block. It contains 1,160 apartments and 73 shops, and even has its own zip code: it was a real turning point in terms of high-density housing. The large S-shaped façade stands out from São Paulo's congested city centre, and connects the city via an indoor shopping street. In both of these Brazilian projects, the rigid forms of the modern movement were adapted to suit the topography, the local climate and the landscape, and the buildings became organic elements with their own unique identity.

The "Towers in the Park" and "Building as Street" models fully converged at the 1957 Interbau housing exhibition in Berlin: it included a large-scale urban development operation to rebuild the Hansaviertel district, which had been devastated by the war. This project included several types of housing blocks and cultural spaces around the Tiergarten, and included works designed by fifty-three international architects, such as Walter Gropius, Alvar Aalto, Arne Jacobsen and Oscar Niemeyer. Three decades after the Weissenhofsiedlung was built in Stuttgart, Interbau 57 exemplified the search for high-density buildings, as collective as they are diverse.

According to Aldo van Eyck, neither society nor its architects were capable of producing an aesthetic or a strategy to solve the problems of urban realities and the manifold demands: "If society has no form, how can architects build the counterform?"[4] Van Eyck's critical thinking marked the change from the initial concepts of the CIAMs, which had helped consolidate the modern movement, to the new ideas of Team X, which signalled its end. This shift can be seen in two urban developments by Alison and Peter Smithson in London, namely Golden Lane (1953) and Robin Hood Gardens (1972), the culmination of two

46

decades of attempts to create large-scale housing operations that allow for a sense of identity, a place that the inhabitants can make their own. The competition brief for Golden Lane called for 313 dwellings on a site that had been bombed during World War II. The Smithsons designed "streets in the air" to turn the access corridors into an extension of the homes, as part of a series of strategies so that the building would become a larger system and draw the city into it. Although their design did not win the competition, it was presented by the Smithsons at the 1953 CIAM IX in Aix-en-Provence as an urban system, a megastructure superimposed onto the city's fabric. As opposed to isolated blocks, Golden Lane interconnected pre-existing buildings and roads in a new kind of irregular, interwoven urban grid, in line with a new relational logic. Almost twenty years later, the Smithsons built Robin Hood Gardens [fig. 46], a new urban model for post-industrial areas in which the city was no longer an ideal, uniform project, but rather a seemingly random cumulative process: Robin Hood Gardens was thus an opportunity to establish connections with the elements found in the context. Instead of aiming to build a city of towers surrounded by parks and residential streets, a new generation of architects wanted to connect the new housing projects to the realities of what was already there.

It is no coincidence that the Smithsons presented the Golden Lane project at CIAM IX, the last such congress attended by its founders, before it was handed over to the Smithsons' young Team X. Even the closing event of this CIAM IX — a visit to the Unité d'Habitation in Marseilles that ended with an evening party on its rooftop — was marked by clashes between several members. What initially seemed to be differing points of view on theoretical issues turned out to be deep-rooted cultural and ideological incompatibilities that highlighted the conflicts between different generations, genders and cultures, precisely on the issues that the projects urgently needed to address. The end of the CIAMs and the death, in the 1960s, of some of the leaders of the modern movement — Le Corbusier, Gropius and Mies van der Rohe — represented the end of an era, and marked the start of explorations into new challenges that had nothing to do with the paternalistic role of architecture and the State.

Houses with No Walls

"To imagine one house is to imagine the whole world."

Yona Friedman

In the 1960s, a number of anti-establishment proposals emerged that aimed to rescue individuals from their condition as isolated consumers, bereft of personality. Irregular and curved lines were used in place of the strict grids of functionalism; it was about prioritising street life over more roads for cars; action over the predominance of images; leisure over consumerism and improvisation over rigid plans. These proposals were influenced by the Situationist International, founded in 1957, and by the structuralists, led by anthropologist Claude Lévi-Strauss, who brought the subconscious and the imagination to the fore. Another key inspiration was philosopher Gaston Bachelard; in *The Poetics of Space* (1957),[5] he blamed mass production for sabotaging the dreams inherent to human beings. The book is a psycho-spatial portrait of the house, based on spaces such as basements and attics: the modern movement had dismissed these spaces as useless, but Bachelard considered them indispensable for the assimilation of our memories and desires. His text played a key role in raising awareness about the effects of spatial experiences, and not forgetting the past and the identity of the inhabitants. The house thus began to be regarded as a broad system, an intrinsic part of dreams. This encouraged an architecture that would enable more intense interactions between people, with greater relevance placed on encounters and fortuitous events.

Three utopian projects initiated in the second half of the 1950s exemplify the search for more complex societies in a new alliance between creativity and technology. None of them showed any interest in the formal presence of buildings, but

47

rather in offering flexible structures for versatile worlds, appealing to the unpredictability of life.

Firstly, New Babylon (1956-74) [fig. 47], by Constant Nieuwenhuys, consisted of a large lightweight roof for a communal dwelling that would not differentiate between art and life, nor between the conscious and the subconscious. It was initially called Dériville, and followed the postulates of the Situationist International founder, Guy Debord, in "Théorie de la dérive" (1956).[6] Nieuwenhuys imagined an anti-capitalist world of transformable structures for a new human being who would enjoy mobility and adventure: the rational *Homo sapiens* would be replaced by *Homo ludens*, "the playing human being". In New Babylon, the land would be owned collectively, and endless driftings and interpretations would become possible: "A territory for nomads on a planetary scale."[7] Nieuwenhuys — who had worked with Gerrit Th. Rietveld, and was influenced by the De Stijl movement — believed that a spatial rupture was not just about the constituent parts of a house (i.e. walls, slabs and roof), as the Dutch group had suggested almost four decades earlier, but rather it was about designing a system of dwellings and services on a 3D mesh that could accommodate a wide range of programmes. This dynamism embraced the whole structure of the city and its potential for interaction to ensure that people would get involved in the creation of their environment. Nieuwenhuys imagined a new social type, the neo-Babylonian, who would freely inhabit collective spaces.

48

The second project is Yona Friedman's Spatial City [fig. 48], like an expandable and multi-layered 3D maze that would provide new housing and recreational programmes. The idea was to build a large umbrella or hanging cloud to host flexible spaces and thus guarantee the future of cities. Shortly before Spatial City, Friedman had worked with Jean Prouvé on a prefab cylindrical housing project, which gave rise to the idea of a structure with stackable dwellings. From Prouvé he learned the logic of prefabrication, and from Konrad Wachsmann he borrowed the connecting system for the pieces, i.e. the scientifically perfect joints that would permit infinite combinations. This solid technical foundation mean that Friedman could present his diverse ideas as something feasible, not only utopian. He imagined variable scenarios within flexible geometric structures that would provide food and shelter for every inhabitant.

In 1956, Friedman presented his studies of variable tetrahedral structures at CIAM X, in Dubrovnik. Soon after, he designed the Spatial City in response to three issues addressed at the Congress: 1) how to regenerate obsolete parts of cities without demolishing them, 2) how to build new ways of living and moving around, and 3) how to redefine the relationships between the house, the street and the city. In 1958, Friedman founded the Groupe d'Études d'Architecture Mobile (GEAM) with Frei Otto, an expert in lightweight structures, to create a mobile architecture that could adapt to the changes in lives. Friedman called for immediate, reusable dwellings, interconnected by public transport, to create non-determined and non-deterministic infrastructure. For Friedman, the city should be composed of variable spaces connected to a permanent framework with two types of uses: "lightweight" (houses and offices), inserted into the structure, and "heavyweight" (roads, services and industry), set beneath the 3D mesh. He also promoted the users' "right to personality" — in line with the democratisation of clothing and the production of "half-finished" cars — and he tried to create a "variable habitat" in keeping with the increased leisure time made possible by modernity. His focus was on the provision of accommodation for the 1.5 billion poorly-housed human beings in the world, but his approach was far more radical than the satellite-town solutions, which he called cities of the elderly, and he criticised the absurdities of modern ideas: "Most of Cité Radieuse's inhabitants in Marseilles don't know each other. Why are they living together?"[8]

Friedman proposed new forms of coexistence as an alternative to the obstructive character of the urban planning trends at the time. To that end, he developed the "property for use" concept in his utopian project Kahn-City (1965), which was organised like a big hotel. When an apartment was empty, a vacancy sign would light up so that it could be inhabited by anyone, and adapted by them too: the user would carry a set of slides in their pockets to project the desired decor. Friedman regarded the house almost as a projection, an image without fixed ob-

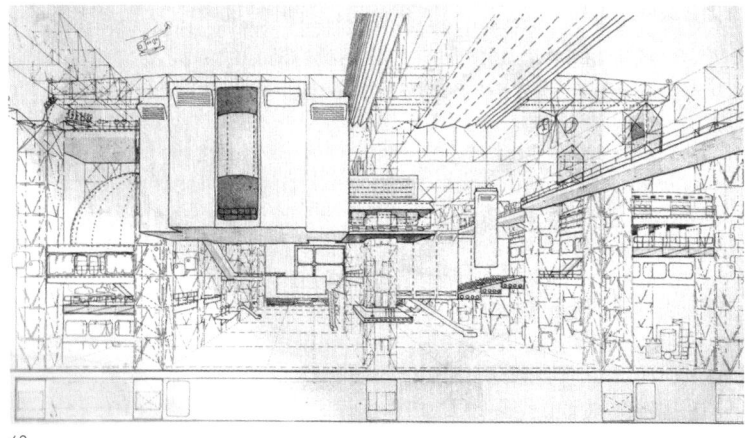

49

jects or owners. A few years later, he designed a typewriter-like device to make houses (Flatwriter, 1969), consisting of 53 keys representing room choices so that anyone could assemble their home to match their personality and print out the plans of their prefab home in a few minutes, to be placed inside the great space of the Spatial City. His idea was to produce customised homes on the basis of algorithms that used the logic of the newly-invented computer programmes.

The third and final project to be discussed here is Cedric Price's Fun Palace [fig. 49], completed in 1961 after a decade of work. It is an adaptable structure with cranes and metal platforms, much like the ones found backstage in theatres. Price imagined it as "a kit of parts, not a building", and he created it with theatre director Joan Littlewood, known as the mother of modern theatre, who inspired Price to design structures that anticipated people's needs. Fun Palace was designed to be a "laboratory of fun", a multi-programme, flexible, technology-based stage that would produce a machine with changing scenes; Price wanted to replace the conventional notion of architecture (i.e. as a sheltering structure) with the logic of an adjustable system, including mobile partitions based on the logic of the *non-plan*.⁹ Price's structure was not subject to the constraints of physical elements, so it could be adapted to suit the requirements of each user. Fun Palace was not designed for any particular location, but rather as a limited-time toy, built to last fifteen years and to be constantly revised by a committee which included Littlewood and Richard Buckminster Fuller, among others. Price worked on this proposal following his own experiences: there was not much room for manoeuvre in his tiny London flat, where his bathtub had to double up as his desk and dining table.

These utopian projects were based on an anti-determinist, non-formal and anti-architectural logic: designs for houses without walls, or houses that disregarded the idea of the family, in schemes that encouraged an intensification of cities. Urban centres were envisaged as flying carpets or mobile roofs, so that each inhabitant could write the script of their own life. All three projects were explained in sections, models and collages to give a realistic angle to their authors' city fantasies and to build bridges between the technical and the playful. Each one outlined infinite possibilities for a drifting world that rejected the fictitious material happiness of the homogenised world, in line with Debord's theories, expounded in *The Society of the Spectacle* (1967).[10] This book was one of the cornerstones of the May '68 uprising that began in Nanterre: at the time, this was the location of shantytowns in Paris, where 14,000 people lived in deplorable conditions. The social revolts that began there spread to other parts of the world, in protests against government authoritarianism and people's lack of control over their own lives. As a result, utopian projects like these ones soon caught on, aiming to create alternative, autonomous societies in which people could identify with their surroundings.

Personal Capsules

"The house is an appliance for carrying with you, the city is a machine for plugging into."

David Greene

The 1969 moon landing was seen as a metaphor for the access to new worlds by means of technology. It inspired the production of inflatable houses and instant bubbles where life could be reinvented. The 1960s and 70s saw the emergence of many counter-culture movements, the goals of which included the creation of microcosms that would ensure human survival and a spirit of individuality. These projects were linked to communication technology and the rise of synthetic drugs such as LSD, as well as the search for spontaneous forms of bringing together alternative identities, such as the hippie movement, which emerged from the rejection of authoritarianism. Some of the most prominent architectural teams who proposed hypothetical worlds included Superstudio, Archizoom, Ant Farm and Archigram. Their common denominator was a desire to expand the universe to embrace any kind of life. So, they developed an architecture without clients or specific sites: radical projects based on the imaginaries of pop art, land art, *arte povera*, the ready-made and collage. Underlying these ironic proposals were theories by philosophers Umberto Eco and Herbert Marcuse, along with a rejection of both the capitalist system and repression. Instead of designing architecture for specific clients, these four collective studios used experimental methods to reclaim areas that were considered to have been hijacked by the political powers. Their work included performances, installations, photomontages, exhibitions, media art and industrial design; they used guerrilla strategies, and deployed architecture as a vehicle for political action or cultural transgression.

50

Superstudio and Archizoom were founded in 1966 in Florence, following the massive flood that covered the city with water. They proposed different ways of occupying land, without the divisions generated by private property. Superstudio — Adolfo Natalini, Cristiano Toraldo di Francia, Alessandro Poli, Gian Piero Frassinelli, Roberto and Alessandro Magris — designed systems like the Catalogue of Villas (1969), for varied conditions and personalities, and the Continuous Monument (1969) [fig. 50], an endless strip to allow inhabitants to appropriate the environment. This concept was carried over to the Parete Castelli system (1973) [fig. 51], i.e. a wall of shelves to store beds, kitchens and tables and thus create infinite environments in a repetition of fractal patterns (a term that was coined precisely at that time).

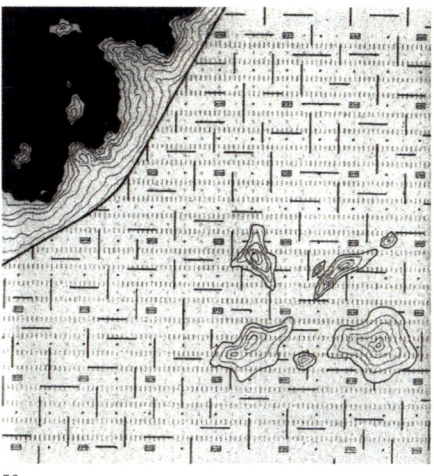

51

52

In 1969, Archizoom — Andrea Branzi, Gilberto Coretti, Paolo Deganello and Massimo Morozzi — presented No-Stop City [fig. 52], an infinite grid without form or façade, based on the fact that new technology made centralised cities unnecessary. This project was a critique of the consumer system. It envisaged constantly improvised uses, as if the world were a gigantic car park for houses, where humans could get by with just a few tents and some packaged food.

Designing open structures implied encouraging free customisation and mobility: Archizoom sought to replace architecture with furniture, providing greater flexibility to systems that could be easily replicated. Andrea Branzi sums up his work as follows: "Making architecture does not just mean making houses or building useful things, but expressing oneself, communicating, inventing with architectural tools and conditions, just as making love means not just producing children but communicating through sex."[11]

Ant Farm, a group founded in Texas in 1968 by Chip Lord and Douglas Michels, designed portable inflatable structures that could instantly colonise a territory. One of their most famous works is the House of the Century (1973), a phallic homage to NASA's designs, built near Houston in collaboration with Richard Jost. This spaceship-like ferrocement structure was parked in a pristine landscape. Although at first it might look like a kind of cross between Frederick Kiesler's Endless House and Alison and Peter Smithson's House of the Future, both of which were designed for exhibitions, the House of the Century was a real dwelling for a client and a future that had already arrived. This house celebrated the use of plastic material, metal and neon lights, and featured a continuous surface of sculpted wood that connected the floor to the furniture. It's like something out of Stanley Kubrick's *A Clockwork Orange* (1971), part of which was filmed in Skybreak House (1966), designed by Norman Foster, Richard Rogers, Wendy Cheesman and Su Brumwell in the United Kingdom under the influence of Richard Buckminster Fuller, the great inspiration for the architecture of all these groups.

Archigram — founded in London in 1963 by Peter Cook, Warren Chalk, Ron Herron, Dennis Crompton, Michael Webb and David Greene — tackled projects as if they were critical metaphors, linked with the ideas of their masters Reyner Banham and Cedric Price. One characteristic feature of Archigram's work was its intense use of technology and the design of mobile structures for nomadic inhabitants. The Archigram members developed different projects: Peter Cook designed Plug-in-City (1964), a city of prefab houses plugged into a megastructure; Ron Herron's Walking City (1964) consisted of robot houses on legs; David Greene's Living Pod (1967) was a prototype stackable cave-house that could even be assembled on the moon; and Mike Webb's Suitaloon (1967) was a pneumatic house-suit inspired by astronaut survival kits.

All of these groups, and their thought-provoking designs, changed people's understanding of the minimum requirements for survival, as well as the concept of lightness in architecture and the connection between the house and the surrounding environment. They proposed new forms of urbanisation thanks to a revised hierarchy between design and furniture.

An exhibition at the MoMA, New York, entitled *Italy: The New Domestic Landscape* (1972),[12] curated by Emilio Ambasz, presented a novel universe composed of flexible modular furniture, adaptable living cells and capsule beds, with conceptual work by nearly twenty Italian architects and designers. The intention was not to speak of houses, but rather "domestic landscapes"; that is, to encompass everything related to living, along with a desire to reconcile the different scales of objects and spaces. Furthermore, the 24-hour daily routine would become a ritual: micro-environments and micro-events were proposed as a kind of setting for domestic life, as a way to reassert the ceremonial nature of everyday actions. In the exhibition, design ceased to be an object and became a platform that questioned the concepts of privacy and territoriality. In the new landscapes by Superstudio and Archizoom, and the habitable artifacts designed by Ettore Sottsass, Joe Colombo and Gaetano Pesce, among others, Manhattan was imagined as a city without the buildings of the past, a large-scale infrastructure for adaptable domestic environments. The exhibition detected the potential of regarding the territory as a domestic space that could be used temporarily by anyone. Additionally, it encouraged a new role for design and architecture: they would become tools to transform the relationships between objects, spaces, people and the environment.

The best example of domestic architecture understood as a landscape made up of technology and design is the Nakagin Capsule Tower (Tokyo, 1972) [fig. 53] designed by Kisho Kurokawa, a member of the Japanese Metabolists. The 140 inhabitable minimum cells, attached to a central service mast, were designed to be an adaptable structure, although during

53

the fifty years of the building's life its configuration was never actually modified. The cells, measuring 4 × 2.5 metre in plan, and produced in steel in a workshop, were assembled on site using cranes. There were eight different typologies, so that individual people could live in a dormitory building, as if it were a space station anchored to the ground. There is no distinction between furniture, walls, the bathroom and technological devices; everything is part of a continuous surface, a kind of futuristic cave that feels like somewhere between a hotel and a scientific experiment. It took just thirty days to build, becoming a materialisation of the Metabolists' desire to construct flexible megastructures as an adaptable system. This notion was popularised at the Expo '70 in Osaka, precisely where Yona Friedman presented his aforementioned Flatwriter machine.

All these groups saw architecture as a happening and a dialogue that would encourage the creation of hitherto unimagined worlds. Their brief existence — they all disbanded in the 1970s — hints at the difficulty of inventing alternatives to standardised models driven by speculation. Nevertheless, their success represented the collapse of top-down, global governance; thanks to them, there were now fresh ideas about how to democratise space, as part of a critical search for flexible structures that people could identify with.

The Inhabitant as a Specialist

"All power to the users."

John F. C. Turner

The late 1960s and the 1970s were marked by the social upheavals of 1968 and people's yearning to regain control over their lives, far from the impossible promises of politicians. The priority was to reestablish the natural balance between people and the environment, to reclaim the sense of identity destroyed by the monotony of mass production. Three key figures encouraged individuals' participation in their habitat by means of more inclusive, humane processes: N. John Habraken, Bernard Rudofsky and Christopher Alexander.

Habraken's critique was that industrialisation could not be used wisely, because the user was excluded from the process. He claimed that the problem had begun in 1918, when standardised housing regulations were propagated as canon: the professional's reductionist approach was incompatible with the instinctive habits of the user, who wanted something different. So, Habraken suggested that the inhabitant and the house could be regarded as one entity. Society could not allow its houses to be taken out of its hands, especially when other solutions were possible: as many solutions as there are people in the world. He claimed that there was nothing worse than living in places that were indifferent to the user's actions. In *Supports: An Alternative to Mass Housing* (1961)[13] he called for "support structures" or frames for prefab dwellings guided by the user's own criteria, a kind of *à la carte* house [fig. 54]. His system, described as "open building", consisted of fixed components — that is, the support (structure and installations) — and variable parts (the infill), which would allow users to participate in the creation of their homes, and customise their

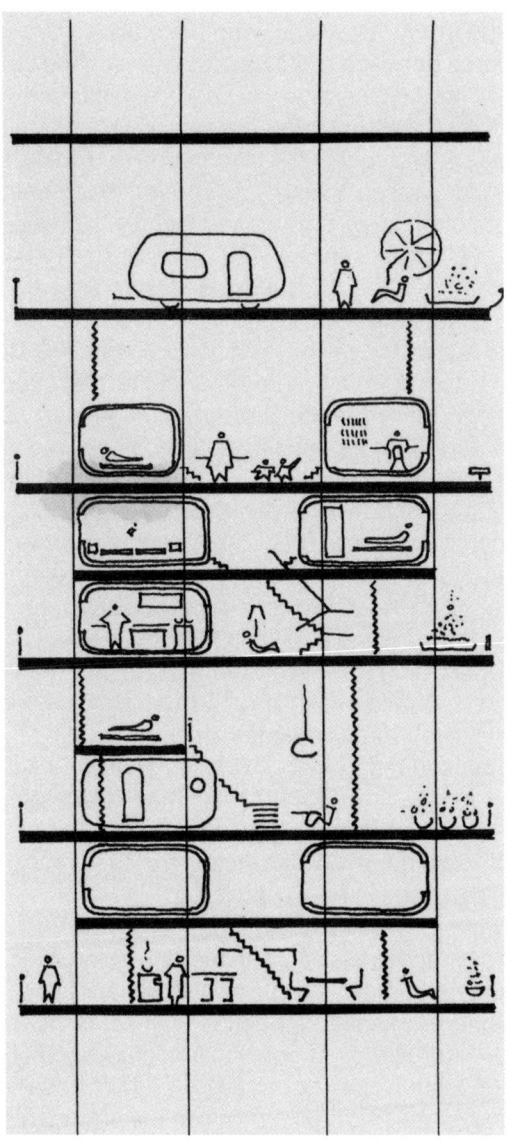

54

Identity

space with products available on the market. This would reduce the distance between producers, designers and consumers, thus bridging the gap between needs and desires.

Habraken saw the architect as an intermediary between the occupant and technology, someone to translate the inhabitant's desires into reality, according to the manufacturing possibilities. His book contained no images: it was not intended to present a formal solution, but rather a methodology, which made it hard to apply. Only 40 copies were sold in the year following its publication, and it took nearly a decade for the first edition to sell out. It became known as "the book that no one has read but everyone has commented on", but decades later, it became a cult reference and Habraken's ideas were regarded as a new paradigm for housing design. There was much criticism of his desire to develop a new language, a kind of Esperanto of construction, and also that his methodology would be very difficult to put into practice, since his approach involved a reorganisation of the building industry. Habraken's research was purely analytical, far from the utopian visions by Nieuwenhuys, Cedric Price and Yona Friedman. Even so, Habraken's "support" and "infill" were similar to Friedman's "heavy uses" and "reduced uses". Three years after the publication of his book, Habraken designed a house-building system that involved reused beer bottles. His Heineken-sponsored WOBO ("World Bottle") allowed walls to be made from stacked bottles, like bricks. Although he only built one prototype of this model house, it was a point of reference in the 1970s for the reuse of existing resources in house-building.

"A dwelling contains at least one whole life",[14] Habraken explained when discussing the need to understand architecture in a more comprehensive way. Many opposed his ideas and considered them solely philosophical matters, however Habraken addressed not only the housing shortage, but also the lack of adaptability that made dwellings obsolete shortly after being built. This cast doubts on the efficacy of architects, and highlighted the work of anthropologists and sociologists, who were more focused on users.

Even the MoMA — an institution established 35 years beforehand, in New York, to exhibit modern work by outstanding creators — held an exhibition about traditional anonymous constructions: *Architecture Without Architects* (1964), curated by Bernard Rudofsky. Two decades earlier, Rudofsky had launched a crusade against the fleeting fashions that led to useless envelopes: he sought coherence between practical needs, lifestyles and clothing. His interest culminated in a rediscovery of the values of vernacular architecture, architecture without pedigree, which he highlighted in the exhibition. The exhibition catalogue[15] featured images of the age-old wisdom of vernacular architecture, from villages in the Sahara desert built using large canvases to the thatched shelters ("palapas") that Kenyan nomads would carry on their backs. The central thesis of *Architecture Without Architects* was that true innovation could be found in these examples, not in industrialised architecture. Its criticism was directed not only at the architects who hindered human development, but also at the West's reductionist view of the rich cultural history of humanity. The catalogue presented architectures in danger of extinction, and celebrated the human skills that modern architects had so foolishly disregarded for decades.

Paradoxically, the book's great tour of the world was actually based on photos found in libraries, cultural institutions, embassies and tourist offices. The most exotic, remote scenes photographed by Rudofsky himself were from villages in Italy, France, Portugal, Spain, Greece and Turkey, showing his somewhat skewed view of unfamiliar "other" worlds.

The 1960s and 70s saw the biggest population increase in the world's history. In 1975, the planet reached 4 billion inhabitants. It had taken us many thousands of years to reach the first billion, 125 years to grow from 1 to 2 billion, and then just 15 years from 3 to 4 billion. In 1976, faced with this alarming situation, the United Nations organised Habitat I, the first global Conference on Human Settlements. It would address the estimated challenge of having to build more than 600 million new dwellings in the following 35 years,[16] an unprecedented scale that required new solutions to deal with the threats facing humanity and nature.

Christopher Alexander summarised this population increase with the following phrase: "Every month, enough human beings to make a city the size of Detroit [1.5 million inhabitants at the time] are added to the world's population."[17] In *A Pattern Language* (1977),[18] Alexander guided readers through the building process to help them develop their own language based on the infinite possible combinations of the different parts that make up a house. He wanted to organise people's needs and instincts using the same logic as computer programmes (new at the time) when they order chaotic structures. In contrast to "artificial cities" like Levittown, he proposed the revival of "natural cities" built by their own inhabitants over time, such as Siena and Kyoto, both famous for their human scale and adaptability. In doing so, Alexander made the picture-postcard vision of Rudofsky's book compatible with the lessons learned from self-construction.

This renewed focus on spontaneous forms of construction partly originated in the work of John F. C. Turner, a distinguished housing philosopher. He was one of the first to point out the qualities of informal constructions in developing countries. For Turner, "when housing is defined as a problem, a housing-problem industry emerges whose mere existence is a guarantee that the problem will never go away".[19] Omitting the user from the process was too obvious a risk at a time when people were becoming increasingly conscious about the fact that events in remote areas had an impact on a shared world, that the planet's resources were finite, and that poorer nations and even minority groups could alter the overall balance. *The Limits to Growth* (1972),[20] drafted by a group of analysts at the Massachusetts Institute of Technology (MIT), was instrumen-

55

tal in raising awareness about the planet's limited resources, the need for shared responsibility by all, paying attention to specific local situations and the widespread use of renewable resources and technologies in architecture.

These aims were implemented in the UN-sponsored Experimental Housing Project (PREVI, Lima, 1969-73) [fig. 55], where architects from four continents gathered to build a low-cost district on a human scale, in which the building process borrowed from local knowledge according to the users' changing needs. PREVI began with an international design competition with no single winner: instead, it brought together thirteen Peruvian designs and thirteen foreign proposals for prototypes in a low-rise, high-density neighbourhood. The participants included Christopher Alexander, Charles Correa, several members of Team X (including Aldo Van Eyck, Georges Candilis and Shadrach Woods) and the Japanese Metabolists Kiyonori

Kikutake and Kisho Kurokawa, all under the leadership of Peter Land. Nearly 500 houses (a third of the number originally planned) were built in 24 types of clusters, with a central boulevard, a school, shops, recreational areas and broad pavements to restore the human character of the streets. Prefab systems and local techniques and materials were used, as well as circular windows, lattices and curved walls. Some houses had two courtyards, others three; some house resembled those of a traditional village, while others were like small-scale industrial workshops. PREVI was a collective demonstration of housing production using non-hierarchical and non-authoritarian systems. It was a mix between the systematised and the adaptable that evolved in line with the identities of the inhabitants. Today, nearly half a century after they were built, it is hard to distinguish the authorship of the original houses.[21] PREVI was considered a milestone in world architecture, but since then, there has been no other large-scale collaborative initiative that took into account the key role of typological and material experimentation as well as the inhabitant's participation in the construction of their own habitats.

Philippe Boudon's *Pessac de Le Corbusier* (1969)[22] is relevant in this regard. The book revisits the 70-or-so houses designed in 1926 by Le Corbusier for the model district of Pessac, and documents the alterations made to them by the occupants over four decades. Pessac is a good example of a single architect defining an entire district with uniform gestures, and Boudon's book contrasts the opinions of users and specialists. It is the first study to highlight the mismatch between the architect's intentions and the inhabitants' transformations (such as smaller windows, gable roofs above the original flat ones and new balconies). Speaking at the official opening of Pessac, Le Corbusier stressed that his intention was to build a standard modulation that could adapt to the personal tastes of the inhabitants. Near the end of his life, however, he also acknowledged, with regards to this project: "Life is always right: it is the architect who is wrong."[23] Boudon's book was published five years after Le Corbusier's death, and coincided with the start of the PREVI project, which from the outset tried to make allowance for the changes that the users would inevitably go on to make.

Since then, collaboratively-designed housing projects have been smaller-scale, isolated efforts. Three examples come to mind, to be described below: the Moduli system in Finland, by Kristian Gullichsen and Juhani Pallasmaa [fig. 56]; Christopher Alexander's Mexicali project [fig. 57], in north-west Mexico; and the Segal method, designed in London by Walter Segal.

The Moduli system by Gullichsen and Pallasmaa is a framework, formed by a modular grid, to combine standardised prefabricated elements: it was a reinterpretation of Walter Gropius and Konrad Wachsmann's panel system, and took the Japanese tatami measurements as inspiration, so that every user could put together their own home like a customisable jigsaw puzzle. Around fifty houses were built with this system, mainly near Helsinki, but production came to an end amid the 1970s oil crisis.

Christopher Alexander's experimental complex in Mexicali, for self-built houses, was a model of community living based on his pattern system: the aim was to blur the boundaries between designer and builder. Although this project was never fully completed due to financial issues, five houses and a community centre were built around courtyards, using inexpensive local materials and solutions such as soil-cement blocks made on site and vaults made with wooden lattice strips, burlap sacks and chicken-wire mesh.

Walter Segal built two housing complexes in London: one with thirteen homes on Walters Way [fig. 58], and another with seven on Segal Close [fig. 59]. These projects were designed to be built economically, without elaborate plans or experience, and using standard timber items available from any DIY store. The system would let the inhabitants express themselves, and

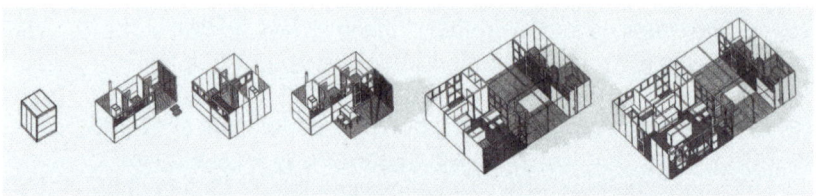

56

57

reflect the distinct qualities of each site: this explains why the two neighbourhoods look so different.

All of these projects broke new ground in terms of improvised innovations for the do-it-yourself housing concept, at a time when the demolition of buildings to erect new ones was beginning to be regarded as senseless. This was the point when non-professional, manual DIY techniques received widespread acceptance in small-scale initiatives, using elements that could serve different purposes and people. On the basis of these principles, the Open City [fig. 60] was built in the 1970s on coastal dunes in Ritoque, Chile, by Amereida, a group of artists, writers, philosophers and architects linked to the Pontifical Catholic University of Valparaíso. The communal houses, built

58

59

Identity - The Inhabitant as a Specialist 161

60

using locally available scrap material, were designed to be spaces for experimentation, manual labour, personal interpretations and a broad range of sensations, evocations and utopias. The Open City's architecture was understood as an action, like writing, walking or reading. This license to include unexpected elements would later on define the architecture of the period, characterised by the search for identity through a range of references, at a time of global uncertainty.

The Bedroom as a Neighbourhood

"The sewer in my house runs through the whole world and transforms in conjunction with those of others."

Álvaro Siza

Cities grew dramatically between the late 1960s and early 1980s, leading to an increase in traffic problems and social breakdown. In response, several housing projects tried to re-establish a more humane sense of neighbourliness by combining high population density with the positive features of traditional villages, aspiring to make places with a unique identity and a sense of community. This approach — that is, creating buildings like little towns within the wider city —fostered privacy, openness and individuality.

In 1966, two seminal books — Aldo Rossi's *The Architecture of the City*[24] and Robert Venturi's *Complexity and Contradiction in Architecture*[25] — promoted the idea that complex ways of living were by no means evils to be vanquished, but rather the driving forces that could lead to more complete solutions. While Rossi placed the house at the heart of urban planning theories, and stressed the importance of the collective nature of the domestic space, Venturi advocated for greater variation in the transitions between the public and the private (as opposed to one-way functionality) while also linking different periods and styles. Rossi and Venturi opened the door to the exploration of more diverse combinations and a greater appreciation of complexity, a trait that characterised postmodern architecture.

At this time, numerous projects encouraged community participation, with pedestrianised estates and typological variation, forming complexes that were both uniform and diverse in character. Solutions had to be as functional as they were labyrinthine. The Honeycomb complex (Casablanca, 1952), built

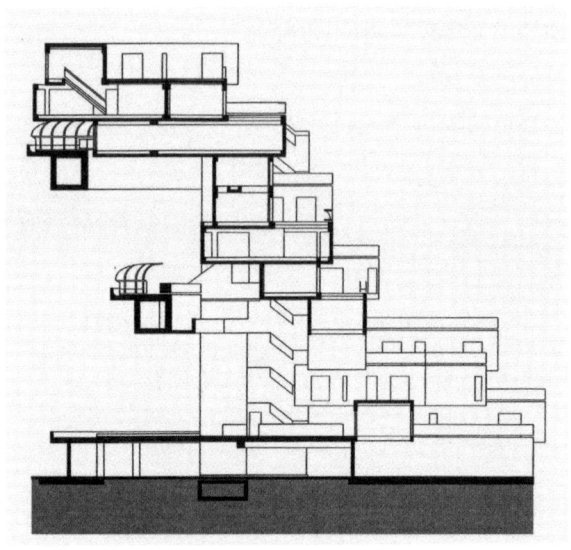

61

by Georges Candilis and Shadrach Woods, was a forerunner to these kinds of residential projects. It is no coincidence that these two young collaborators of Le Corbusier at the Unité d'Habitation in Marseilles were members of Team X, and highly critical of the inhuman nature of modern architecture. Both belonged to the Groupe d'Architectes Modernes Marocains (GAMMA), a faction of the CIAMs. Their analysis of Casablanca, presented at the CIAM IX in 1953, was unlike the other presentations at the congress. Instead of focusing on the parameters of modern architecture, they presented a study of slums and owner-built houses, in order to learn from the everyday conditions of the local inhabitants. They were clearly ahead of their time: they looked into spontaneous architecture a decade before Bernard Rudofsky, John F. C. Turner and Christopher Alexander did so. Their designs for low-cost Honeycomb houses offered varied typologies, prefab elements and courtyards. For Candilis and Woods, the real builders of the city were the ordinary people; the architect's job was simply to articulate the different voices and the public and private spheres.

Seven designs exemplify this new role of architecture: Moshe Safdie's Habitat 67 complex in Canada; Ralph Erskine's Byker Wall houses in England; Ricardo Bofill Taller de Arquitectura's Walden 7 complex and Francisco Javier Sáenz de Oíza's El Ruedo, in Spain; Charles Correa's Tara houses; Balkrishna Doshi's Aranya housing in India; and Álvaro Siza's Quinta da Malagueira district in Portugal.

The first example, Safdie's Habitat 67 [fig. 61], was built for Expo 67 in Montreal and it consists of 158 apartments formed by 354 prefab units. The dwellings, with different sizes and layouts, have private terraces and are staggered to generate a changing topography, as if it were a hill of randomly stacked houses. With the motto "a garden for everyone", the project emerged from the need to provide the privacy of a house surrounded by nature, but within an urban context.

In stark contrast, Erskine's Byker Wall development (Newcastle upon Tyne, 1969) [fig. 62] is a nearly mile-long undulating strip of variable height, with balconies, outdoor corridors, pre-existing constructions and almost a dozen different typologies. Whereas Habitat 67 achieves its variety by rotating or separating the same type of block, Byker Wall does so by using different languages for its 9,500 inhabitants, echoing the irregular character of the old district and its uneven topography. It fosters a neighbourhood spirit by employing unusual elements such as differently coloured bricks, metal walkways and different shapes that reflect the variation of typologies. For Erskine — who lived with his family in a small cottage that was also his studio — the relationship between a house and its surroundings was a fundamental theme, which is why his project in Newcastle is an ensemble of small worlds. Byker Wall was designed with a sense of appropriation and a DIY-like aesthetic. It took more than a decade to complete the construction, and Erskine moved his studio to the site so that he could involve the local community in the

63

62

project and ensure that it reflected the varied character of its inhabitants.

Like Erskine, Ricardo Bofill moved next to his Walden 7 project (Sant Just Desvern, Barcelona, 1975) [fig. 63], and one of his main collaborators, his sister Anna, still lives in Walden 7. They borrowed the project's name from the novel *Walden Two* (1948)[26] by American behavioural psychologist B. F. Skinner, who in turn borrowed it from Henry David Thoreau's *Walden*. However, Skinner was by no means extolling a solitary life based on Thoreau's mythical hermit, but rather he was referencing his real life: Thoreau could not have survived in the woods without the help of his neighbours, relatives and guests, thanks to whom he had a home, food and company. Skinner's novel was not inspired by isolated fictional lives, but rather by the realities of social coexistence. The setting for his story was an egalitarian commune of 1,000 inhabitants subject to a new family model not defined by blood ties. With this idea in mind, they designed Walden 7, a building/mountain composed of 446 dwellings for new forms of coexistence, in a small cosmos of apartments arranged around patios, terraces, shops, communal spaces and walkways with rooftop swimming pools. This massive fortification — red on the outside, and blue and yellow in its numerous inner courtyards — combines surrealist influences with local architecture. As with other housing complexes by Anna and Ricardo — such as Kafka Castle (Sant Pere de Ribes, 1968), the Gaudí district in Reus (1970) and the Red Wall (Calpe, 1973) — the origins of Walden 7 can be found in The City in Space (1970). This (unbuilt) project was the first in which they sought to create labyrinthine communities of stacked dwellings that resemble a north-African *kasbah*: The City in Space featured fortress-like houses that emerged from the varying relations between stairways, corridors and extensions. Each house — despite its small size — was a world unto itself.

El Ruedo ("The Bullring"), (Madrid, 1986-91) [fig. 64] designed by Francisco Javier Sáenz de Oíza, is a microcosm of 350 dwellings curving around a large central courtyard. The outer façade of its huge spiralling wall is in solid brick with small windows, thus turning its back on the heavy traffic, while the inward-facing façade has a colourful geometric pattern. El Ruedo and its "living wall" was designed so that the inhabitants could have a space of their own: these social dwellings were built for families, rehoused here in a ghetto that the police dared not enter for decades. A television programme filmed the handover of the houses to these families, and it shows the difficult task of fulfilling their desires, which in many cases were contradictory. For instance, there was a couple with eight children, and they had been moved into a pair of two-bedroom flats; others spoke of the dubious usefulness of a built-in wardrobe when they owned no clothes other than what they had on. The programme recorded Saenz losing his temper after listening to the complaints of the inhabitants, responding to one of

64

the owners: "You should move out, and become an architect. Let's see if you could do a better job!"[27]

In India, Charles Correa's Tara homes (Delhi, 1978) and Balkrishna Doshi's Aranya (Indore, 1989) both focus on embracing diversity. The former is a complex of terraced dwellings, a kind of hill of houses that open onto a long central courtyard, while the latter is a cluster of 60 low-cost adaptable houses, arranged around small courtyards, with a communal logic and strong identity not often found in self-built projects. Both architects made the most of the high-quality manual labour on offer, and they used lattices, open corridors and terraces, according to their deep understanding of the local climate and customs. Doshi found inspiration in *How the Other Half Builds* (1984),[28] by architecture critic Witold Rybczynski: it was a manual on building techniques, applied to the developing world. The book's title is a reference to another one written almost a century before by Jacob A. Riis, *How the Other Half Lives* (1890),[29] discussed in the first chapter. Rybczynski's manifesto not only

65 66

acknowledges the existence of other worlds, but also defends the idea that inhabiting and building are part of the same process, just as Martin Heidegger, N. John Habraken and Christopher Alexander had understood it, albeit in different ways.

A perfect example of long-term involvement with a community, and in connection with the place, is Álvaro Siza´s Quinta de Malagueira district in Évora, Portugal [fig. 65], which began in 1977 and went on for decades. The neighbourhood has a similar ambiance to a traditional village, but accommodates all the expected modern services. The design resembles his social housing community in Bouça (Porto, 1975) [fig. 66], providing a sense of shelter despite being right inside the city. Both of these designs by Siza create microworlds, and incorporate the changing needs of the users and of the city. They take up Henri Lefebvre's contemporary defence of the "right to the city"[30]: the need for a social space for everyone, a right that is not about possessing something, but rather building the city's spaces based on the experiences of its dwellers.

67

68

The works described in this section completely transformed their localities and created a sense of identity in the neighbourhood. They were modern settlements, unlike those in the standard manuals: these projects reflected complex narratives based on profound realities, and were characterised by their high population density, the provision of public zones and the interaction between diverse voices. In short, they were monuments to the community that lived in them; they emphasised the identity of the inhabitants, becoming a symbol of a place.

Other works from that period also reflected this fostering of diversity and communal initiatives, including the following seven projects: Hassan Fathy's New Baris Village (Kharga, 1967); the apartment blocks by Aldo Rossi and Carlo Aymonino in Gallaratese (Milan, 1972) [figs. 67 and 68]; Hubertus House by Hannie and Aldo van Eyck in Amsterdam, a temporary home for single parents and their children; the mixed-use complex in Ivry-sur-Seine (1969) on the outskirts of Paris [fig. 69], by Reneé

69

70

Gailhoustet and Jean Renaudie, which includes the apartment where Gailhoustet lived for decades; the Barbican Estate (1971) in London, by Chamberlin, Powell & Bon; Dawson's Heights (1972) by Kate Macintosh; and finally Alexandra Road (1978) by Neave Brown.

Gailhoustet's creativity is visible in the way housing becomes part of the city, and it extends through balconies, terraces, squares and open corridors. Ivry-sur-Seine, along with the Barbican Estate, is one of the most exemplary projects of this era. The Barbican Estate [fig. 70] took almost three decades to complete, has 2,000 homes, a concert hall, cafeteria, theatre, museum, library, cinemas, parking and a Tube station. It explores the varying relationships there can be between houses and public space — there are ponds and quiet gardens, lively terraces and apartment towers inserted in the urban fabric, as well as different housing typologies related to the cultural life supplied by the complex — as if it were its own world.

71

Dawson's Heights, designed by Macintosh, was a manifesto in favour of expressing the individuality of the homes. Influenced by this project, Alexandra Road [fig. 71] prioritises pedestrian walkways, and the design of different typologies that extend the dwellings by means of terraces and balconies. The complex has a central pedestrian street, and forms a new topography in order to turn its back on a railway line. In turn, the cars go underground, making the houses seem as if they were on a hillside. Like the other examples in this chapter, these were not buildings, but rather landscaped neighbourhoods or islands brimming with identity, despite having been built in generic contexts or empty landscapes.

---

[1]   Jacobs, Jane, *The Death and Life of Great American Cities*, London: Pimlico, 1961.

[2]   Boesiger, Willy (ed.), *Le Corbusier: oeuvre complète 1946-1952*, Zurich: Girsberger, 1953, p. 186.

[3]   Le Corbusier, *La Ville Radieuse*, Boulogne-sur-Seine: Éditions de l'Architecture d'Aujourd'hui, 1935.

4   Aldo van Eyck, quoted in: Frampton, Kenneth, *Modern Architecture: A Critical History* [1980].

5   Bachelard, Gaston, *La Poétique de l'espace*, Paris: Presses Universitaires de France, 1957 (English version: *The Poetics of Space*, New York: Orion Press, 1964).

6   Debord, Guy, "Théorie de la dérive", *Les Lèvres Nues*, 8-9, Ambers/Brussels, 1956.

7   Nieuwenhuys, Constant, "L'intensification de l'espace", in Duvignaud, Jean (ed.), *Nomades et vagabonds*, Paris: Union Général d'*Éditions*, 1975.

8   Friedman, Yona, *L'Architecture mobile*, Paris/Tournai: Casterman, 1958.

9   See Littlewood, Joan, "Non-Program. A Laboratory of Fun", *Drama Review*, vol. 12, no. 3, New York, 1968. In Hardingham, Samantha (ed.), *Cedric Price Works 1952-2003. A Forward-Minded Retrospective* (vol. 2), London/Montreal: Architectural Association/Canadian Centre for Architecture, 2016, p. 93.

10   Debord, Guy, *La Société du spectacle*, Paris: Buchet-Chastel, 1967 (English version: *The Society of the Spectacle*, New York: Zone Books, 1995).

11   Brazi, Andrea, in Various Authors, *Arquitectura radical* (exhibition catalogue), Las Palmas de Gran Canaria: CAAM, 2002, pp. 10 and 16.

12   Ambasz, Emilio (ed.), *Italy: The New Domestic Landscape. Achievements and Problems of Italian Design* (exhibition catalogue), New York: The Museum of Modern Art, 1972.

13   Habraken, N. John, *De dragers en de mensen. Het einde van de massawoningbouw*, Amsterdam: Uitgaven, 1961.

14   Ibid.

15   Rudofsky, Bernard, *Architecture Without Architects* (exhibition catalogue), New York: The Museum of Modern Art, 1964.

16   See Alexander, Christopher; Davis, Howard; Martínez, Julio and Corner, Don, *The Production of Houses*, New York: Oxford University Press, 1985, p. 11.

17   Chermayeff, Serge and Alexander, Christopher, *Community and Privacy. Toward a New Architecture of Humanism*, Garden City: Doubleday & Co., 1963, p. 13.

18   Alexander, Christopher et al., *A Pattern Language: Towns, Buildings, Construction*, New York: Oxford University Press, 1977.

19   Colin Ward, preface to Turner, John F. C., *Housing by People. Towards Autonomy in Building Environments*, London: Marion Boyars, 1976, p. 4.

20   Meadows, Donella H. et al., *The Limits to Growth: A Report for the Club of Rome's Project on the Predicament of Mankind*, New York: Universe Books, 1972.

21   See García-Huidobro, Fernando; Torres Torriti, Diego and Tugas, Nicolás, *Time Builds!*, Barcelona: Editorial Gustavo Gili, 2008.

[22] Boudon, Philippe, *Pessac de Le Corbusier: 1927-1967, étude socioarchitecturale*, Paris: Dunod, 1969.

[23] Ibid., p. 1.

[24] Rossi, Aldo, *L'architettura della città*, Padua: Marsilio, 1966 (English version: *The Architecture of the City*, Cambridge (Mass): The MIT Press, 1984).

[25] Venturi, Robert, *Complexity and Contradiction in Architecture*, New York: The Museum of Modern Art, 1966.

[26] Skinner, B. F., *Walden Two*, New York: Hackett, 1948.

[27] Exchange captured in a TV programme, *No te mueras sin ir a Ronchamp (Sáenz de Oíza)*, RTVE, broadcast on 26 December 2014. www.rtve.es/alacarta/videos/imprescindibles/imprescindibles-no-mueras-sin-ir-ronchamp-saenz-oiza/4881972.

[28] Rybczynski, Witold, *How the Other Half Builds*, Montreal: Centre for Minimum Cost Housing, 1984.

[29] Riis, Jacob A., *How the Other Half Lives: Studies among the Tenements of New York*, New York: Charles Scribner's Sons, 1890.

[30] See Lefebvre, Henri, *Le Droit à la ville*, Paris: Anthropos, 1968.

Coexistence

This chapter focuses on the end of the twentieth century and the start of the twenty-first, looking at buildings that try to bring together opposing characteristics — individual and communal, virtual and tangible, rural and urban — and highlighting the multiplicities that make up our world. These projects were designed to resolve the incompatibility between the speed of change and the immobility of what is built, and also the discordance between houses and the desires of their inhabitants.

Throughout history, the house has been the greatest laboratory for architectural experimentation, but it has also been the ultimate redoubt of conventionalism. The house embodies both a projection towards the future and an attachment to the past; it is a pronouncement of values and a formula that reflects habits; a shield and a mirror at the same time. Faced with this diverse range of realities, all the projects gathered in this section strive for a sense of coexistence in the varying relationships between buildings, people and the territory.

Five sections summarise the quest for diversity, not only in terms of users but also of environments, budgets and worldviews. The first section discusses the collapse of the universal model of the modern home, and includes breakout architectural and artistical projects. The second section presents Japanese houses that have expanded structural, material and spatial possibilities; the third deals with "porous" housing complexes that express variety, while the fourth section looks at what happens between one room and another by considering housing projects that respond to environmental challenges; the fifth and final one addresses recent cooperative and social housing projects. All the projects in this chapter reflect the idea of plurality, in a new take on people's participation in the creation of a shared habitat. They all emerged in reaction to monofunctional housing models, and they all offer alternatives in order to redefine the relationship between living and working on the basis of new concepts of family, ownership and use.

One consequence of taking our most private activities into the public sphere, and the infiltration of the outside world into our private lives through telecommunication, has been that the house is no longer a space of interior privacy. Simultaneously, the entire outside world can now fit inside any house of any size. The solutions discussed in this chapter, all designed to broaden the definitions of coexistence and cohabitation, question the very meaning of "my house", and they reinterpret what it now means to live together and alone, prioritising the things we share.

The Destruction of the House

"The inhabitants of this architecture, those strong enough to love it, would become its voluntary prisoners."

Rem Koolhaas and Elia Zenghelis

Between the 1970s and 1990s, the destruction — partial or total, accidental or intentional — of four emblematic projects in different parts of the world triggered a crisis in the mass housing model. By that time, housing developments had grown enormously in scale — as had criticisms of it. All four complexes — the Pruitt-Igoe (St Louis, Missouri), the Nonoalco-Tlatelolco complex (Mexico City), the Oriental Masonic Gardens neighbourhood (New Haven, Connecticut) and the Bijlmermeer residential complex (Amsterdam) — had initially been praised as great achievements, but over time they were neglected, and in some cases they even exacerbated social segregation. In fact, it would seem that their very structure fostered such problems.

The Pruitt-Igoe complex (1954) designed by Minoru Yamasaki, was one of the biggest housing complexes in the United States, with nearly 2,800 homes in 33 eleven-storey towers. It was also one of the most expensive, costing 60% more than the national average for public housing. Despite being praised, at the time of its construction, as a model for eradicating slums, Pruitt-Igoe was demolished in 1972, less than two decades after it opened.

The Nonoalco-Tlatelolco complex (1964) [fig. 72] in Mexico City was designed by Mario Pani for 100,000 inhabitants as an example of modern housing with public spaces and communal services. It was the scene of grave incidents, including a student massacre in its central square just four years after it opened. Also, several of its buildings were destroyed in 1985 by two earthquakes.

72

73

74

The Oriental Masonic Gardens neighbourhood (1971) [fig. 73] was built by Paul Rudolph near Yale University. It was supposed to be an example of affordable prefab housing, but was demolished ten years after completion due to protests by its occupants, who felt as though they were living in stacked, leaky railway carriages.

The Bijlmermeer district in Amsterdam was designed in the 1970s by Fop Ottenhof, as part of a masterplan by Siegfried Nassuth to house 50,000 people. It soon became one of the most starkly segregated neighbourhoods in the Netherlands: half of its inhabitants were unemployed, and 90% earned less than the country's average minimum wage.[1] The poor living conditions in the large, mass-produced suburbs, even in supposedly exemplary cities, were laid bare when a plane accidentally crashed into one of the Bijlmermeer buildings in 1992. One of the first to warn about the misconceptions of the Bijlmermeer project was Jakoba Mulder, an architect and urban planner who advocated for the creation of public parks in the new districts and proposed children's play areas every hundred houses. Mulder strongly disapproved of the Bijlmermeer design, which consisted of 90% tall blocks and 10% low-rise buildings. Unfortunately, her counterproposal (with lower buildings of varying heights) was rejected, and her criticisms about the lack of integration built into the chosen design were not made public until the 1980s.

Pruitt-Igoe was a turning point in architecture: the neighbourhood's demolition was televised, signalling a change in housing policies and the cancellation of the large-scale repetitive projects which had in fact aggravated economic and racial divisions. Nonoalco-Tlatelolco marked the demise of governmental responsibility and support for large-scale social housing schemes, and housing solutions were thus left in the hands of private developers. Oriental Masonic Gardens brought an end to the optimism that had emerged from architectural experimentation with prefab housing, while Bijlmermeer [fig. 74] helped raise public awareness about the need to restore the social and urban fabric through designs that connect housing to public transport, have built-in communal services and encourage mixed uses. Rather than demolish the Bijlmermeer, it was renovated in 2017 by NL Architects and XVW architectuur; they left the interiors incomplete, to be finished off by the residents, and they focused their efforts on reorganising the collective spaces. It was a manifesto of the potential of reusing existing buildings.

These examples show four different responses to similar issues: 1) total demolition, 2) the end of publicly-funded housing projects provided by the welfare state, 3) the end of low-cost housing experimentation and 4) the transformation of obsolete housing in order to restore community life. Part of the problem with all these complexes, and thousands of others like them based on the same precepts, was that they were conceived as small worlds in which coexistence was inextricably linked with conflict.

In the latter decades of the twentieth century, the physical or conceptual destruction of these serial housing models gave rise to new alternatives, grouped under the label of post-structuralism and deconstructivism. One major influence came from the theories of French philosophers Jacques Derrida, Roland Barthes, Gilles Deleuze and Julia Kristeva, who were interested in the fragmentary nature of reality and "otherness". These thinkers proposed a literary deconstruction based on the recomposition of the meanings of things: it was about separating the object (the text) from the meaning, or rather inverting hierarchies and avoiding binary thinking in order to foster conjunctive thinking and allow for the inherent contradictions of life. In essence, "either this or that" was rejected in favour of "this, that and everything". In the field of architecture, this led to a dismembering of the components of buildings, whereby unexpected relationships were established between the different parts. It was a matter of bringing in that which, historically, had been excluded or considered marginal. If architecture had been striving for centuries to project an image of utility, unity and certainty, now attention turned to exhibiting its fisures.

Three architects linked to academic institutions in the United States — Peter Eisenman, John Hejduk and Lars Lerup — proposed the deconstruction of the house by taking apart and recomposing the core elements of architecture. These three architects — all born roughly around the time of MoMA's *International Style* exhibition (1932) in New York — had grown up under the umbrella of the rigid postulates of the modern movement, and felt they had been left with "little air to breathe". They did not try to rebuild the world, but rather they wanted to make all possible worlds coexist.[2] Their ideas took the form of drawings and models that changed the way architecture was represented, and their designs became a critique of the architectural discourse.

For years, Lerup worked against the single-family house, defined by him as "morality manifested in form". He sought to recover its condition as a complex entity, a dream-machine that requires active participation by its users. His drawings included disjointed angles that expressed the mismatch between desires and reality, as a way to highlight the incompatibility between family narratives and houses' activities and forms. As he saw it, architecture should no longer try to hold back the forces of such contradictions, but rather display the ruptures and allow conflicts to coexist in order to understand them as something natural.

In *Planned Assaults* (1987),[3] Lerup proposed three "attacks" on architecture, via three houses: in the Nofamily House, he questioned the domestic routines based on blood ties; in Texas Zero, he reinvented the house based on the needs of an independent woman; and in Love/House, he played around with the concept of waiting, in a house that stretched out time to expand the limits of perception and provoke the imagination as an essential function in the home. In all these projects, Lerup challenged the standard narrative associated with the house. Love/House, for example, was to be used for fantasies and lovers, and Nofamily House was a critique of the fragmentation of the domestic realm into sectors: the space for the man, the space for the woman, the space for the girl and the space for the boy. Lerup's designs included doors that served no purpose, handrails that escaped through the house and stairs that led to nowhere. Like in Jorge Luis Borges' short stories, Lerup would redefine the meaning of a window, an entrance or a step: this way, people would stop for a moment and interrupt their daily activities, thus making room for the more real and overlooked aspects of human existence. Lerup's desire was to shake up the house-dwellers: he wanted to make them question the passive relationships they had with seemingly inert objects like armchairs, mirrors or walls, and deconstruct architecture with all its fantasies and its ghosts. In short, he wanted to discover more complete coexistences.

Hejduk spent several decades designing abstract houses that worked as arguments to reinvent architectural elements and how they were combined. One Half House and House 10 (both designed in 1966) and the Texas, Diamond and Wall series (1954-73) gave rise to new ways of representing spaces, so they could be imagined in different ways. Hejduk's house drawings would include infinite games of composition, so that each element would be independent. Pillars, planes and volumes thus all became protagonist components, floating in the void: they stopped being structural elements, to become symbolic.

Like Hejduk, Eisenman made no reference to the context, purpose, users or history of his houses. Variations of the same elements were combined; in fact, he saw his process as an endless game of dislocating pieces and their meanings. Eisenman designed eleven houses (Houses I-XI, 1968-80), inspired by linguist Noam Chomsky. House VI (Connecticut, 1975) [fig. 75] has a red staircase that leads to nowhere and hits the ceiling, a pillar that does not touch the floor, and another one right in the middle of the dining room. Meanwhile, in the master bedroom, a gap in the floor prevents a couple from sleeping together in a double bed. By striving to upset the modern movement's form/function dialectic, and show that walls are not partitions but ideas, Eisenman questioned conventions and lifestyles by rethinking the meaning of every single element, from a bathroom to a doorway. Unlike the shoddily assembled house in Buster

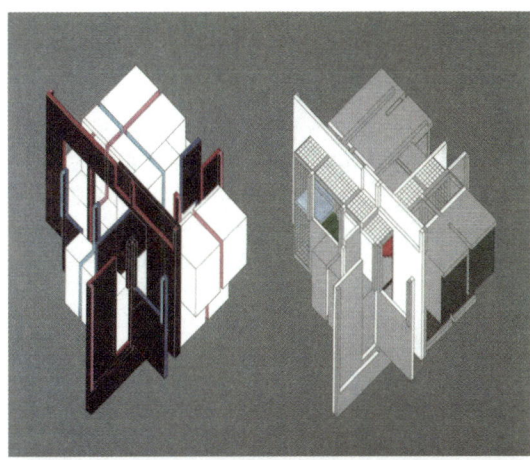

75

Keaton and Eddie Clein's *One Week* (1920), Eisenman expanded the definition of the limit by proving that the solidity of a building does not reside in its built parts, but rather in its concepts.

Nearly twenty years after its construction, Eisenman's House VI gave rise to the book *Peter Eisenman's House VI: The Client's Response* (1994),[4] which brings together a range of opinions on that particular house, from the owner, the architect, critics and writers. Its users had nothing but praise for the house, despite the discomfort caused by some of the design features, such as hitting one's head on the stairs and not being able to add on an extra room during the construction process for a daughter who was about to be born (she had to sleep in a crib in the hallway; Eisenman asked for the crib to be hidden in the garden before the arrival of important visitors). The house had, in the inhabitants' own words, "stretched our imagination" in a "continuous process of learning about form and space" that made all the architect's ideas worth enduring.[5]

Eisenman got to build four of his series of eleven houses (I, II, III and VI), and Hejduk's Wall II house was only built after his death, at a different location and for a different client. Lerup, Hejduk and Eisenman's houses were mostly representations, analyses constantly being reworked: 129 drawings in the case of Lerup's Nofamily House, infinite axonometric projections by Hejduk and countless diagrams for Eisenman's houses. The projects often imagined a theoretical client — almost always an artist or a philosopher — and they were accompanied by explanatory texts that substantiated the conceptual and spatial quirks of the designs. These projects were influenced by the intervention carried out by Charles Moore in his house in New Haven (1965): it had three perforated towers that took over the centre of the house to connect the different levels, to bring in natural light and enhance the way the space played with perspectives and languages. By breaking up the interior space of a traditional home that had no distinguishing features, Moore transformed the house into a discontinuous landscape that could host infinite juxtapositions of symbols.

This rupture of the domestic realm was featured in a small exhibition, *Houses for Sale*, held at New York's Leo Castelli Gallery in 1980. Eight architects exhibited projects aimed at reestablishing the lost link between dream houses and real, built houses. These architects wanted to break free from the limitations of the stereotypical commissions of conservative clients, and thus rethink the house in all its complexity. Emilio

Ambasz proposed making a crack in the ground from which a house would emerge, facing a sunken courtyard. Peter Eisenman designed his house as an axonometric object, a kind of unfolded cube about to take off; Vittorio Gregotti imagined a sequential experience, beginning with long parallel walls that heightened the sense of confinement; Arata Isozaki proposed a sort of mausoleum formed by repeated cubes; Charles Moore designed a house as a container for formal references; César Pelli proposed a narrow corridor that joined independent volumes; Oswald Mathias Ungers put a house inside a house inside another house; and Cedric Price's contribution was a 24-hour living toy house, somewhat like his Fun Palace project, as a way of addressing issues that never appear in conventional architectural programmes such as boredom, envy and ageing. Price saw this as a way to enable the coexistence of opposites like privacy/gregariousness, temporariness/permanence and leisure/action. The exhibition drew attention to the major concerns of an era in which a house now had to take on far more than what had otherwise been acknowledged up to that point.

This groundbreaking trend was consolidated following the *Deconstructivist Architecture* exhibition at the MoMA in 1988.[6] Curators Philip Johnson and Mark Wigley brought together projects by seven architects including Eisenman, Frank O. Gehry, Rem Koolhaas, Bernard Tschumi and Zaha Hadid. Back in 1932, Johnson had curated MoMA's first architecture show, *The International Style*, a renowned exhibition which legitimised modern forms of living. 56 years later, he brought together a new group of architects who were deliberately "violating" the pure forms of Modern architecture. The exhibition catalogue bears some resemblance to the one that accompanied *Houses for Sale* at the Leo Castelli Gallery: one features houses by eight architects, while the other contains projects by seven architects; the former has imaginary houses without clients, and the latter has commissions of a new architecture that was beginning to invade the cities.

Two other houses sum up the paradigm shift of the time, in an attempt to represent the instability of life: Gehry's house in

76

Los Angeles (modified over several decades since 1978) [fig. 76] and Koolhaas's Bordeaux House (1998). Gehry's house was part of the *Deconstructivist Architecture* exhibition, and triggered the start of this trend. It was a collage of cheap materials — metal mesh and grating — that burst into an existing house, turning it into a discourse on its makeshift nature: the violation of spaces and of the traditional house forms. The latter project, designed by Koolhaas for a client who had become disabled, provided moving spaces. A lift turned the centre of the house into a mobile station: the project defied the normal static condition of architecture.

A key influence on the architecture of this era came from the Institute of Architecture and Urban Studies (IAUS) in New York and the periodical *Oppositions* (1973-84). The IAUS had been conceived as an anti-establishment institute, headed by Eisenman and Kenneth Frampton, who in the late 1960s wanted to create a kind of American Team X to define the architectural debates following the demise of the CIAM. Based on this impulse, in the 1990s, architects and theorists from different parts of the world formed the Any Corporation group, under the leadership of editor Cynthia Davidson and the theories of Eisenman and Ignasi de Solà-Morales. The intention was to address new relationships with time (which was no longer linear), place (no longer specific), people (who were no longer like a model inhabitant) and objects (which no longer had a physical reality). The titles of a series of annual conferences, each of which became a book, sum up the group's intentions: *Anyone*, *Anywhere*, *Whatever*, *Anyhow*, *Anyplace*, *Anybody*, *Anything*, *Anywise*, *Anytime* and *Anymore*. The idea was to "problematise" architecture, to make it coexist with complexities to create spatial alternatives to deal with the the unpredictable, for anyone, at any time and place, and in any way.

Four artists — Dan Graham, Gordon Matta-Clark, Louise Bourgeois and Absalon — took on these challenges in their transgressions of the domestic space. In *Alteration to a Suburban House* (1978), Graham replaced the front wall of a house with a huge glass panel that exposed the users' inner life to the public. In *Splitting* (1974), Matta-Clark cut a house in half, releasing it from its confines, similar to how Moore extended the interior space of his home in New Haven. In *The Cells*, a series of installations created over several decades, Bourgeois displayed the innards of houses by singling out everyday objects — doors, stairs and furniture — and presenting them as symbols of repression. Absalon's six *Cells* questioned the interactions between individuals and the world through their belongings, their bodies and their daily actions. His video *Proposition d'habitation* (1991) recorded his experience in one of the individual white cubicles that he had designed with the bare minimum that would allow him to bathe, smoke and masturbate. Unlike Hannes Meyer's *Co-op room*, Absalon's cell is not intended to evoke any connection with the outside. The camera is the only element that interacts with a human being who seems to have no exterior world to relate to.

All these works address the central debates that accompanied the breakdown of the modern stereotypes in terms of housing: Graham blurred the boundaries between private and public; Matta-Clark shattered the seemingly stable image of houses; Bourgeois exhibited imprisonment in the domestic realm; and Absalon emptied the interior, leaving it as an inert space, completely disconnected from the outside, people and history. Bourgeois and Graham's work transgressed the meanings of everyday elements, such as the walls that isolate us, while Matta-Clark and Absalon disavowed the attachment to the permanent. From that moment on, "being at home" meant neither stability nor shelter.

The Immaterial Dwelling

"We can only recognise the *house* by joining several of its functions that are scattered through the city, like if they were pieces of broken glass."

Toyo Ito

Several Japanese homes built in the late twentieth and early twenty-first century epitomised the emerging media-based era in which the virtual and the real would co-exist. Tokyo — the ever-changing epicentre of new technology — was the ideal setting to imagine the domestic space of the new millennium. Toyo Ito used the term "liquid space"[7] to describe the broadening-out of the physical and conceptual limits of digital media, which was opening up new avenues for architecture whereby users could became "modern-day nomads" or "android bodies".

As discussed below, this trend began with the work by Ito that was influenced by his mentor, the Metabolist Kiyonori Kikutake, who had designed floating cities and convertible houses back in the 1960s. The trend then took a new direction with Kazuyo Sejima and Ryue Nishizawa (SANAA), former collaborators of Ito, and later with Junya Ishigami, who started out in Sejima's studio. There is no continuous line of thinking among these architects: instead, they represent ruptures between generations, and even among each architect's own career.
Ito, Sejima, Nishizawa and Ishigami all propose a coexistence between hitherto disparate concepts in their houses: they seek to combine the natural and the artificial, the useful and the contemplative, in a world without demarcations between the physical and the immaterial. As Ito himself put it: "To produce a flow of air between the real and the fictitious space."[8] All the designs are responses to lifestyles that have been fragmented by the breakdown of the cities' continuous spaces.

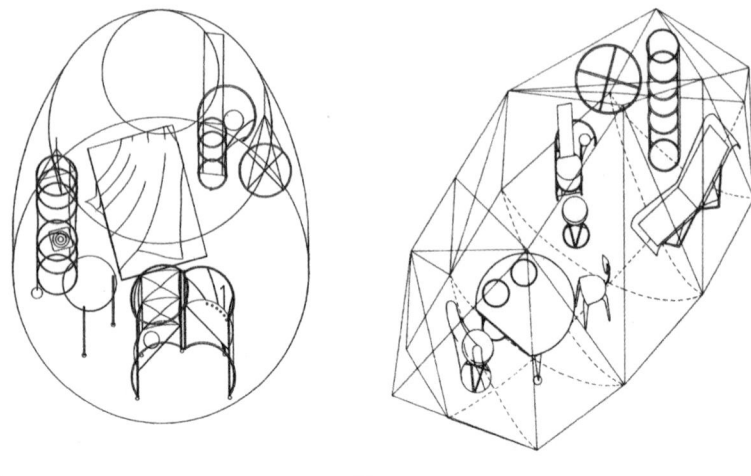

77 78

In Pao I (1985) [fig. 77] and Pao II (1986) [fig. 78], Ito reformulated the meaning of a house for the "nomad women" of Tokyo. Their "home" was scattered around the city; the dining room was a restaurant, the wardrobe was a clothes shop and the garden was a gym. Ito proposed a portable tent/cabin that resembled an inflatable dress, containing a bed, a toilet, a place to eat fast food and an information capsule to navigate around the city virtually (years before the spread of the Internet). These projects are not far removed from the Suitaloon or the Cushicle by Archigram member Michael Webb, or the *unhouse* concept by Reyner Banham, but they involve technology that was thirty years down the road. Ito designed architecture that did not need a physical form. Instead, it appeared as clothing, or as a phenomenon, a fluid ambiance of light, sound and images.

A year after working with Ito on Pao I and Pao II, Sejima opened a studio of her own and challenged her mentor's inhabitable capsules, architectures that "envelop" people, to design alternative places where people could move freely. Platform I (1988) and Platform II (1990) "destroyed the cosmology of the house".[9] They marked the start of explorations that redefined

79

the relationship between interior and exterior, and between structure and furniture. Small House (1999) and House in a Plum Grove (2003) synthesise her ideals: privacy in shared spaces, connection with plant life in a dense urban fabric, and spaciousness in minimal structures. Her architecture does not draw boundaries: instead, it blurs the limits, makes different environments coexist in the same small place, and proposes equitable, non-hierarchical relations between users. Her extraordinarily thin minimal walls and structural lightness facilitated her more elastic concept of privacy. House in a Plum Grove, built for a couple with two children and a grandmother, occupies a floor area of just 6 × 6 metres, in which a slender tower redefines the strict division of domestic space and the concept of privacy. Instead of creating rooms, Sejima built 17 cells with no pre-defined purpose, connected by voids that resembled interior windows to create new relations between the spaces.

For example, in the building with 100 apartments (Gifu, 1998) [fig. 79] on ten levels, Sejima groups together minimal housing cells, many of them with double-height spaces, in var-

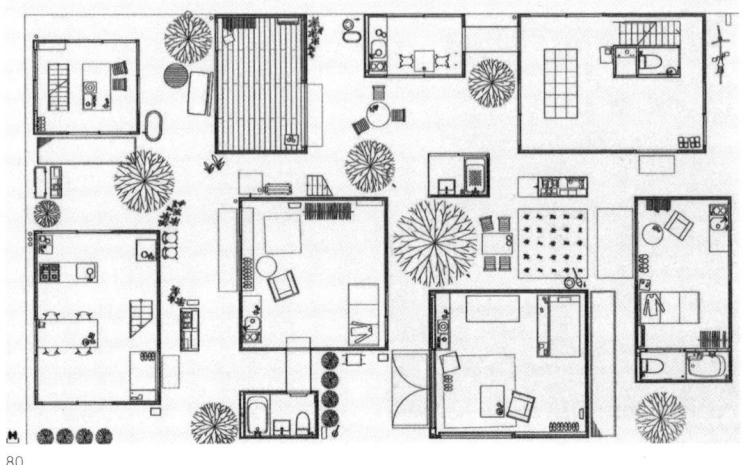

80

ied layouts and connected to a gap/terrace, or a non-defined space, as a way to explore new forms of privacy within collective structures. Another example is Nishinoyama House (Kyoto, 2013), a group of ten houses with a similar layout and scale to the homes in a traditional Japanese neighbourhood, but with courtyards and gardens inserted amongst the 21 fragmented volumes that make up this kind of "exploded" house. By replicating the dense, irregular urban fabric of Japan's vernacular architecture, this cluster of houses makes up a sequence of spaces connected or isolated by voids.

This interest in amplifying what happens between one room and another was taken to the limit by Nishizawa in Moriyama House (Tokyo, 2005) [fig. 80], where he separated each part of the house into different volumes spread out across the plot. The house — built for a son, his mother and occasional future tenants — is composed of volumes of different sizes. One of the cubes, for example, contains only a shower. The outer walls are 5 cm thick, and the interior walls are 1.5 cm thick, which allows for a rethink of its physical and conceptual meanings.

In Garden & House (Tokyo, 2011), Nishizawa designs a series of thin stacked platforms that extend towards the exuberant vegetation on a site that is just 4 × 8 metres in plan, in one of the most heavily congested zones of Tokyo, creating a vertical garden to sleep, play and work in.

Junya Ishigami, who worked with Sejima and Nishizawa (SANAA) at the time of the House in a Plum Grove project, has set out five points to guide the architecture of the twenty-first century: no predefined purposes, no form, no scale, no context and no architecture. In contrast to the five points defined by Le Corbusier almost a hundred years before — buildings on pilotis, free open plan, free façades, roof gardens and horizontal windows — Ishigami proposes a more vague use of architecture's intrinsic materiality, its context and its use, rather than focusing on its compositional elements; he sought to generate a range of events and incorporate the ambiguity between the solid and the ethereal. Ishigami believes that the technical potential of architecture has not really been explored, other than as a fossilised presence. He therefore proposes working on new scales, from the micro (subatomic particles and nanotechnology) to the macro (universe and cyberspace), in order to apply the logic of natural phenomena, such as the structure of clouds or raindrops, to architecture.

Ishigami dilates the space that lies between a void and a partition, and he makes new worlds appear in-between. Natural and artificial, old and new, open and closed: they all coexist in the Home for Elderly People with Alzheimer's Disease (Akita, 2019) [fig. 81]. Here, Ishigami groups the shells of several unused traditional timber houses from different parts of the country, to form a complex that feels familiar to the residents: the architecture evokes their childhood memories in a new large house. It is like a small town for residents who cannot leave, with different kinds of trees and stones of various origins to create a welcoming, recognisable landscape for all the residents. "I would like to define a new sense of comfort that is completely different from the procedure in modern architec-

81

ture", he says,[10] interpreting comfort as diversity. This idea was the starting point for House and Restaurant (Yamaguchi, 2019) [fig. 82], a cave dug into the ground and moulded in concrete. Ishigami seeks to create a receptive architecture that is not only for people but also for nature, animals and insects. "Just imagine how many more types of architecture there can be [...]. Encountering all kinds of individuals. All kinds of groups, things, environments and values. Things we know, things we don't."[11]

The intention to blur the boundaries of the domestic space can also be found in Shigeru Ban's houses. In Curtain Wall House (Tokyo, 1995), the outer walls are replaced by a large Velcro-fastened curtain that constantly changes the users' relation with the outside. Ban seeks to bring together a range of different uses, such as in his Naked House (Saitama, 2000),

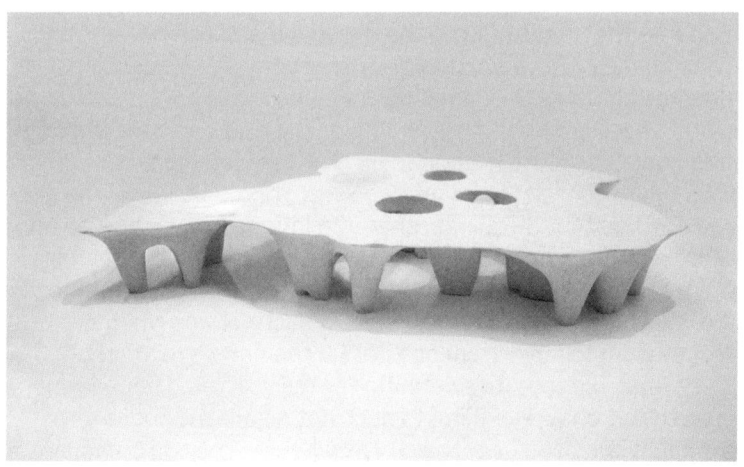

82

a translucent hut containing four cubes on wheels. These mobile rooms can easily be shifted around by their inhabitants to reconfigure their house with each movement. Ban, an expert builder of emergency housing for natural disaster zones around the world, uses lightweigth materials and components made from recycled waste. He does not prioritise form, and he regards the house as an instant shelter: he has thus been able to work with aspects that were previously alien to domestic architecture. More than anything, this approach has led him to question the solid and impenetrable quality of the house, and all the add-ons that come with it: he therefore understands the house in a way that is not attached to forms.

Sou Fujimoto, in turn, expands the interactions between the private and the exterior realms. House NA (Tokyo, 2011) is similar to a tree house, but without a tree: it has a sequence of platforms at different heights, as if they were branches somehow hanging in mid-air. Instead of a three-storey house, as allowed by the building regulations, he took the total permitted volume and distributed it across 20 different interlocking levels. This project exemplifies the term "co-dividual architecture", which respects the needs of both the individual and the collective, in living spaces where typological and programmatic divisions are eliminated. Using the same logic, Fujimoto has constructed two rental apartment buildings in Tokyo. The first one consists of small dwelling units that open up to a terraced landscape made of wood, to connect terraces, walkways and balconies. The second one has four dwellings, split into independent volumes and seemingly stacked at random. It reproduces the typical image of a suburban house, but without their free-standing condition: the inhabitants have to enter and exit each volume whenever they want to move from one part of their home to another. Somewhat like Toyo Ito's definition of the scattered house which opened this chapter, Fujimoto does not regard the house as a complete enclosure, nor the city as a house. The two complement each other, piece by piece. Being at home means entering and departing the city, without being able to distinguish between them. As in the other examples in this chapter, reshaping the dynamics between the different parts of the home generates a new sense of coexistence with technologies, nature and people. In turn, people are no longer defined — paradoxically — by their corporeal condition.

Porous Habitats

"By dwelling we are also talking about shops, schools and public services."

Lina Bo Bardi

In the early twenty-first century, several new projects managed to create a confluence between the local and the global, and between the individual and the communal — not as a way to merge these opposing ideas, but rather to express the realities of the diverse. The most commonly used terms in architecture, "coherence" and "simplicity", lost ground to words like "simultaneity" and "fusion". Under the influence of philosophers Gilles Deleuze and Félix Guattari, architects became interested in the idea of the "fold", i.e. something that separates and unites at the same time to generate multiple exchanges between the interior/exterior and background/figure. This is how buildings came to be episodes that reflect an unfinished condition according to the plural expression of society.

The best example of this phenomenon is the Silodam Building (Amsterdam, 2002) [fig. 83] by MVRDV, a studio founded by Winy Maas, Jacob van Rijs and Nathalie de Vries. Silodam is a shipping-container-like block with 157 apartments, mixed uses and public spaces, built on water. The apartments are grouped into clusters of four to eight units, distinguished from the outside by different finishes and colours. The dwellings vary in size and height, and have different outdoor spaces and types of entrance, through balconies and walkways. The building has a large public terrace at the rear, a dock underneath to allow small boats to enter, several bridges that lead to the apartments and bicycle parking. This huge pier for houses is somewhat reminiscent of Le Corbusier's Unité d'Habitation, but without its desire to impose order. Instead, Silodam expresses a variety of uses, reflecting different lifestyles.

83

Before Silodam, MVRDV built the WoZoCo building (Amsterdam, 1997) [fig. 84], a colourful apartment block of 100 units with cantilevered balconies and seemingly randomly placed windows. The façades of both Silodam and WoZoCo show varying degrees between public, semi-public and private, and they display the typological variation. These same concepts have been applied to another building by MVRDV: El Mirador (Madrid, 2005, with Blanca Lleó) [fig. 85], a block of 150 apartments perforated by a huge void that serves as a raised plaza for the residents. As for the shape of the building, it seems like the architects have taken a normal housing block, arranged around a central patio, and stood it up: the patio now becomes a void in the air.

84 85

MVRDV's influence can be seen clearly in the work of Bjarke Ingels (BIG), particularly in three buildings in Copenhagen — VM Houses (2005, with Julien De Smedt) [fig. 86], Mountain Dwellings (2008) [fig. 87], and House 8 (2010) [fig. 88] — and also in the buildings VIA 57 West (New York, 2016) and Sluishuis (Amsterdam, 2022). Ingels and MVRDV team members Maas and Van Rijs all worked at OMA, and they borrowed from Rem Koolhaas's concept of architecture as a hybrid space; that is, buildings that are something between a house and a loft, between a skyscraper and a courtyard, between a dynamic object and an iconic symbol, and between a building and a neighbourhood. This convergence of multiplicities was underlined in Koolhaas's discourse on the generic megacity, which favours dense but "porous" or permeable buildings with diverse programmes. VM Houses, for example, consists of 209 units with 76 different types, surrounded by collective spaces. VIA 57 West, meanwhile, forms a block with cinemas, shops, a library, a gym and private spaces that open onto an inner garden.

Two architecture firms exemplify the inclusion of more open programmes, in a new interpretation of the building regulations: Lacaton & Vassal and Elemental. In their housing pro-

86

87

88

89

90

jects, Anne Lacaton and Philippe Vassal employ lightweight prefab materials, and they give their buildings an unfinished look, allowing them to build a larger surface area on a lower budget. Their Cité Manifeste (Mulhouse, 2005) [fig. 89] and their units in Saint-Nazaire (2011) [fig. 90] show a simplified architecture, but with complex uses. The economy of means they subscribe to is influenced by agricultural constructions — greenhouses and chicken coops — to add small "extra" spaces inside the houses, through the use of polycarbonate plates and aluminium sheeting. They began this trend in one of their first commissions, Latapie House (Floriac, 1993), where they added a greenhouse frame to an existing house to create a

91

kind of transformable shed that could be adapted to the user's changing need for light, transparency and ventilation.

Lacaton & Vassal, together with Frédéric Druot, consider older buildings as existing resources that should be reused. They have even proposed alternatives to the French government's 2003 policy of demolishing supposedly useless apartment blocks.[12] Their projects prove that renovating these types of buildings is less costly and faster than building new ones. Their transformation of the Bois-le-Prêtre Tower (Paris, 2011) [fig. 91] is a good example of this potential: they have added a new space to each of the nearly 100 apartments in an obsolete 1960s block, by means of a glasshouse-like space attached to the façade, thus extending and personalising the dwellings. Furthermore, the tower was renovated without having to vacate the apartments, and this "double skin" has created a new 3-metre-deep gallery that halves energy consumption and cuts noise.

Elemental Studio, headed by Alejandro Aravena and Andrés Iacobelli, heeds the lessons of incremental growth in housing and aims to expand the potential of open spaces. Their designs for Quinta Monroy (2004) and Colonia Lo Barnechea (2014)

92

93

[fig. 92] in Chile, as well as houses in Monterrey, Mexico (2010) [fig. 93], feature unfinished "half-houses" which the users themselves finish off, over time. In Aravena's own words, it is a matter of designing "a house that is so porous that extensions could be made within the pores and the actual structure, inscribed in the silhouette of the volume".[13]

The works discussed in this section reflect a new kind of role for architects, as if they were the developers of underutilised land. Also, there is a new perspective on regulations, which are no longer considered hindrances, but rather platforms that can facilitate more interactive lives, in which the strength of a project lies in its capacity for synthesis: dock houses, lookout towers and mountain houses. The best examples can be found in six paradigmatic works: La Mémé (Brussels, 1972) by Lucien Kroll; the homes on Genter Strasse (Munich, 1972), designed by Otto Steidle and Doris and Ralph Thut; the Ökohaus (Berlin, 1987) by Frei Otto and Herman Kendell; the Nemausus building (Nimes, 1987) by Jean Nouvel; Next 21 (Osaka, 1993) by Yositika Utida; and Frauen-Werk-Stadt (Vienna, 1995) built by a group of women under the leadership of Franziska Ullmann. These

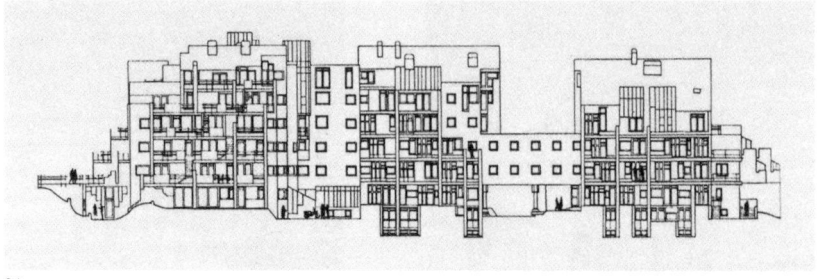

94

projects wanted to bring about real social transformation, and their creators conceived utopia in a realistic way.

La Mémé [fig. 94], the student complex for the Medical Faculty, in Brussels, was built following a participatory process. For Kroll, the building was concluded on the day the structure was erected. The rest was simply a natural process of personal adaptations, as seen on its irregular façades. The housing scheme on Genter Strasse seems to have an improvised character, but the homes are resolved in a way that does not compromise on privacy nor suffocate the spaces.

Ökohaus [figs. 95 and 96] is a participatory experiment of 18 low-cost dwellings. It represents a shift in the role of the architect, who becomes the orchestrator of distinct, often opposing forces (i.e. market interests, urban regulations and diverse individual desires). This "three-dimensional garden city" is made up of a collection of different houses that form part of the same tree-like structure. Otto's objective was to heighten the interaction between people and their habitat, and relegate the architects to the role of tool-creators for the construction of open structures, encouraging a coexistence between opposites. The Ökohaus was part of the 1987 Internationale Bauausstellung (IBA) in Berlin; continuing the tradition begun by Interbau 57, i.e. to rebuild the Hansaviertel district in Berlin. In fact, the IBA designed a ten-year reconstruction programme for several areas via the insertion of quality housing into the urban fabric. The 1987 exhibition featured housing projects by Aldo Rossi, Álvaro Siza, Charles Moore, John Hejduk, Peter Eisenman, Oswald Mathias Ungers, Herman Hertzberger and Zaha Hadid, among

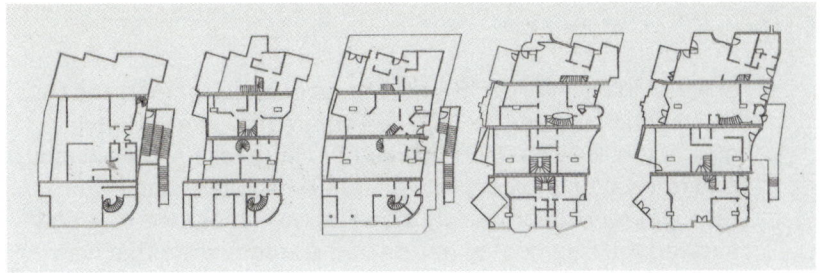

95

96

Coexistence - Porous Habitats 207

others. Unlike Interbau 57, held three decades earlier, and the Weissenhofsiedlung six decades before that, the underlying idea of the IBA was to bring together new designs (IBA Neubau) and renovation projects (IBA Albau). This understanding, in favour of renovation, slowly made its way across the city, and showed the fragmented nature of the architecture that was built in the following decades.

With the Nemausus apartments, Nouvel transformed the brief to build 40 m^2 homes: he made them 40% larger by lowering costs, as a result of using prefab industrial materials and open walkways. In this case, its somewhat "unfinished" appearance did not mean a poor-quality construction, or that the neighbours would be hearing each other through flimsy walls. Here, the homes — arranged on different levels, according to a range of apartment types — have double-height spaces and open onto generous verandas.

In the Next 21 building, Utida commissioned different architects to design 13 of the 18 homes in the complex. And this variety did not stop at the façade, as is commonly the case, but rather it was the result of a truly open programme, designed so that modifications could be made easily, even to installations. In the Frauen-Werk-Stadt building — Margarete Schütte-Lihotzky was one of the judges for the competition — everything revolved around making care work and domestic chores as simple as possible. The complex has a daycare centre, pharmacy, police station, shops, public spaces, sports facilities, shared laundries and recreational areas on the roof-top terraces. It is a building designed to create good pedestrian routes and connect the surrounding neighbourhoods. In these six projects, the concept of porosity is not manifested in any formal solution, but rather it is present in the uses and in the relationship with the city and among the people.

The logic of "porous" and unfinished buildings runs the risk of generating a romantic vision of the free appropriation techniques of informal architecture: precarious solutions can have dangerous consequences. One project that illustrates the dark side of these dynamics is the transformation of the David Tower in Caracas, an unfinished and abandoned 45-storey office building located in the Venezuelan capital, which was illegally occupied: it housed over three thousand people. This improvised building, praised in international architectural circles, reveals solutions created by squatters, people who cannot afford to wait for answers from architects and governments, answers that never come. However, this vision hides the story of those residents who died or were injured when they fell from the building's unsealed openings, or fell down staircases without railings, in this unfinished vertical favela.

A similar case was the demolition in 1993 of the Kowloon Walled City in China. It was the most densely populated place in the world, and called the largest human anthill: it had over 1.255 million inhabitants per square kilometre (for comparison, Seoul or New York have under 20,000 inhabitants per square kilometre), and its destruction was advertised as a solution. Kowloon was the prime example of how housebuilding can in fact perpetuate social injustice, and its recent transformation into a park seems to be a success. However, the new solutions — giant towers full of substandard housing, built in the peripheries of Hong Kong or wherever in the world — continue to stoke the discussions on the limits to density that the demolition of the Pruitt-Igoe complex seemed to have resolved. The new massive complexes contravene regulations with the logic of the "favelisation" of the world, a result of housing being left to the free market.

Between One House and Another

"Between the house of childhood and the house of death, between the house of entertainment and the house of work, is the house of everyday life that architects have called by so many names: home, house, dwelling, etc., as if life were to take place in a single place."

Aldo Rossi

In the first two decades of the twenty-first century, alternative housing ideas arose with the aim of doing less harm to the ecosystem and society. Interest was focused not only on the houses themselves, but on their outward ramifications. Two strategies highlight the extremes of these explorations: one is based on the technical performance of minimal housing, and the other on the potential of the users' improvisation. The former entails the creation of prototype self-sufficient cabins, according to the lessons of Richard Buckminster Fuller and Jean Prouvé, while the second can be exemplified by the Japanese collective houses that follow the logic of capsule hotels (a mini-cabin for sleeping), but blur the boundaries between the public and the private spheres, according to the line of work pioneered by SANAA to offer new formats for shared living.

Four examples of the first strategy stand out: Renzo Piano's minimal Diogene cabin [fig. 97] — built for Vitra at its Weil-am-Rhein headquarters, and ready to be transported by helicopter — with solar panels and a rainwater tank; Norman Foster's Habitats for Mars, designed to be produced using 3D printers; the Ikea house, marketed as low-cost prefab furniture; and the Wikihouse, a digitally-manufactured building system with open-source technology to democratise access to adaptable housing. These initiatives — all of them utopian, except for Piano's — are committed to the creation of minimum spaces

97

to reduce the environmental impact and improve the economic model of housing.

The second strategy emerged from shared housing experiences in Japan. It seeks to bring in other types of functions not associated with the domestic sphere and can be summed up in two examples. Firstly, the Yokohama apartments (2009), by Osamu Nishida/ON Design and Erika Nakagawa, have a courtyard that resembles a large semi-public foyer, designed to be a place for exhibitions, resting and working. Four stairways lead to the four tower-dwellings, each of which has its own private bathroom; the apartments are like tents placed within a kind of urban tree. The second example is the LT Josai shared occupancy house (Nagoya, 2013) [fig. 98], by Yuri Naruse and Jun Inokuma. It consists of thirteen rooms, laid out like a 3D maze

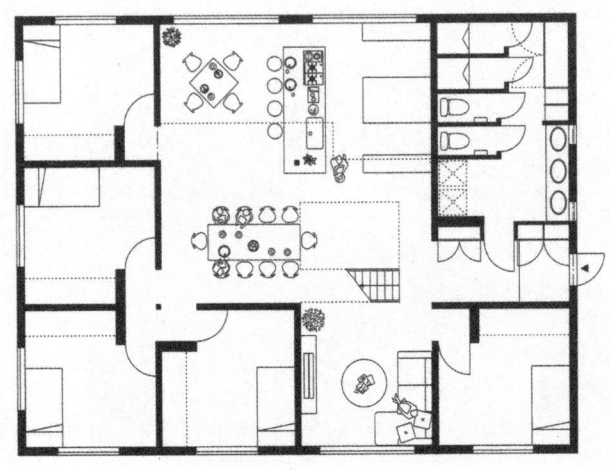

98

that generates overlapping common areas and private rooms, allowing each inhabitant to use this shared structure in different ways. The design encourages improvisation, and its uses are to be defined by those who live there.

In the face of ecological and social emergencies, the work of a group of women architects (as described below) in different parts of the world, especially in places characterised by inequality, offers alternatives that combine the two strategies referred to above. They hope to find a middle ground between deferring to technology and harnessing the potential of the inhabitants' own skills. The proposals focus not only on reducing the pollution produced by buildings and the construction industry — which accounts for 36% of the planet's energy consumption and 39% of its carbon emissions — but also on improving all aspects of construction: materials, working conditions and preservation. To achieve this, they propose decentralised production processes and community participation, against capitalism's destructive ways of managing resources.

These designs are far from the high-tech capsules of Piano or Foster, and are closer to Hassan Fathy's earth architecture and the disposable cardboard houses designed by Guy Rottier in the 1960s. Rottier, after working for Le Corbusier in the Unité d'Habitation of Marseille and founding the GEAM group with Yona Friedman, designed "clandestine" architectures that tried to undermine the dogmas of modernism: they were small utopias, made of rubbish and manipulated topography, that reflect his life philosophy of "live after tomorrow".

Concern about the after-effects of constructions, as well as the potential in reusing available materials, is visible in the work of Anna Heringer. This can be seen, for example, in the rural housing she designed for peasant families in Bangladesh, made collectively with compacted earth and straw; in her projects for the largest refugee camp in the world (Rohingya, where around 860,000 people live); and also in the bamboo shelters built in China. The goal is to achieve, in Heringer's own words, "better and broader solutions, at a lower cost, for a larger number of people".[14] To that end, she sets out seven principles in the *Laufen Manifesto for a Humane Design Culture*: collaborating eye to eye, designing work, unfurling beauty, identifying the local, understanding the territory, educating designers, and shaping policy.[15]

This desire to reclaim the ancestral knowledge of vernacular architecture is not about a picture-postcard vision of simpler solutions, in line with a colonialist or paternal gaze — instead, the aim is to consider how older approaches might inform new kinds of collaboration. The following examples reveal this: the houses built with raw earth, by Mariam Kamara in Niger; Marina Tabassum's refugee camps and affordable bamboo housing prototypes for flood emergencies in Bangladesh [fig. 99]; and the houses for orphans built by Anupama Kundoo in India, using mud bricks dried in the sun and then heated with charcoal dust and clay to make them as resistant as possible — the houses can then be turned into a kind of furnace for manufacturing other necessary ceramic products, such as tiles, sinks and even pans.

99

In just three years, from 2011 to 2014, China consumed more cement than the United States did in the entire twentieth century.[16] A nostalgic view of traditional practices can easily become a sense of urgency to include them in any future construction. If that happened, we would be able to come up with other ways of doing architecture, linked to the body, the land, equity and what happens between one construction and the next.

Houses that Cooperate

"What happens when the land problem, the injustice of lack of access to housing, and patriarchal violence intersect?"

Ana Falú

Based on the view that we do not inhabit houses, but rather ecosystems, and given the lack of affordable houses in the world, various cooperative housing and protected public housing projects have sought to challenge the notions of use and possession, in favour of more equitable systems. The two main contributions of twentieth-century housing — the open floor plan, and the open building — are now joined by the desire to remove housing from the free market in order to reestablish it as a human right, associated with notions of care and collaboration. This was underscored by the Covid-19 pandemic, when health problems were linked with housing problems — just like in the early twentieth century, when contagions forcibly led to the reinvention of architecture and cities.

Today, transforming housing is not just about the building itself. Any such change must include subsidies and must respond to temporary and emergency needs; future maintenance must be factored into the design, and the environmental and social effects of the buildings must be taken into consideration. It's about creating houses without housewives, and moving on from thinking that a house is an individual fragment that wastes resources. In this section, the chosen projects are centred on collaborative solutions and reuse. They seek to spend less, achieve more and do no harm. These works are based on the lessons of the social housing projects in Red Vienna (1919-33), and on ensuring that the inhabitants stop being passive consumers.

100

In housing cooperatives, the inhabitants are usually the ones who obtain the land, define the financing models, the regulations and the layout of the spaces, and in many cases they even participate in the building process or in the subsequent maintenance. The first modern housing cooperatives date back nearly 150 years, although they surged in popularity at the beginning of the twentieth century, before a second boom in the 1960s. Today, they play a new role in the face of the climate emergency and inequality.

In Denmark, the first housing cooperative was created in 1866, and currently 30% of the homes in Copenhagen operate under a cooperative regime. In most cases, these are apartments for rent in renovated buildings, but their value has recently been liberalised by opening them up to the free market, which has, in turn, undermined the affordability of the model. This demonstrates that it is not enough just to provide access to affordable housing — in which the total cost and associated expenses must be under 30% of the inhabitant's income — but there must also be measures to ensure that such projects are not mere money-spinners, in order to prevent evictions and the increase of empty houses used only as an investment.

101

The best examples of cooperative housing are those impulsed by the inhabitants, with varied programmes and public spaces. They are mainly found in Europe — especially in Switzerland, Belgium, Germany, Spain, the Netherlands and Austria — while Uruguay and Argentina stand out in the Latin American context. In the city of Zurich, 26% of the population lives in housing cooperatives built through participatory processes.[17] Two complexes there are of particular note: Kalkbreite [fig. 100] (2014) and Zwicky-Süd (2015) [fig. 101]. Both projects are based on three key principles: demonetising housing, connecting it to the city and to community spaces, and making it as varied as its inhabitants.

    Kalkbreite, by Müller Sigrist Architekten for 160 inhabitants, is built on top of a public tram warehouse. It consists of apartments ranging from one to nine bedrooms, studios for rent, shops, cinema, a large central public space, rooftop terraces and a collective house made up of apartments that share a kitchen where a chef does the cooking. This project provides a solution for both the inhabitants and the neighbourhood: the building generates almost the same number of jobs as the

102

103

number of inhabitants it houses. In turn, Zwicky-Süd, built on the outskirts by Schneider Studer Primas, for 260 residents, integrates different activities and economies. Like the Kalkbreite complex, it is not closed to the public: it maintains privacy without excluding. Likewise, it highlights the personalities of the users and amplifies connections with the exterior. In both projects, new links are created between the spaces for rest, shops, socialising areas, service infrastructures and public transport.

This approach can also be seen in the cooperative housing complex built in the Lysbüchel Süd neighbourhood of Basel. It consists of different apartment buildings that share a central garden and common areas, and the complex was created as part of the transformation of a post-industrial zone, promoted by the non-profit foundation Stiftung Habitat. Two new buildings in this complex — the Lyse-Lotte block [fig. 102], designed by Clauss Kahl Merz with Martina Kausch, and Weinlager [fig. 103], by Esch Sintzel — are surrounded by gardens, terraces and balconies, which bring together various activities, programmes and different types of people. The Weinlager building, which is located within an old wine warehouse, offers a sneak peek of an attractive future: abandoned buildings are repurposed by generating new typological solutions which extend the building's existing floorspace. This leads to a rethink about the whole layout, about how to offer shade and integrate uses, such as shared laundries, open corridors, rooftop terraces with vegetable gardens and spaces for rent that contribute to maintenance costs. By reusing the existing structure, there was a 42% reduction in the building's grey energy expenditure. Furthermore, by turning the old pillars into a key protagonist, a feature of the new layout, the buildings acquire an unusual visual appeal. The use of a photovoltaic panel system and a groundwater heat pump means that the building is self-sufficient for two-thirds of its total energy consumption. Each building in the complex — made by different groups of architects — expresses diversity and a sense of adaptability that is largely unexpected in projects of this scale.

In Madrid and Barcelona, in just five years (from 2013 to 2018), housing rental prices rose by 32% and 55% respectively.[18] This has led to the creation of housing cooperatives that challenge the existing private property model. In Barcelona, the work of the collective LaCol stands out, as exemplified in three cooperative projects: La Borda (2018), Sotrac and la Morada (the latter two are under construction). La Borda [fig. 104] has 28 dwellings of different sizes, collective services around a central covered patio and a cooperative shop facing the street. This work was self-organised by the inhabitants, who turned down the option of having an underground car park in favour of

104

105

spaces for shared amenities. The whole project was designed in a way that minimised environmental impact, starting from the construction stage right up to the building's daily use. The project generates a public space in the entrance that links the street with a park, close to the Sotrac housing cooperative. In turn, the La Morada building is a feminist project that expands the definitions of living and the concept of a caring city. In Madrid, the Entrepatios cooperative built Las Carolinas (2021) [fig. 105], a project designed not to suffocate the inhabitants with mortgages or high maintenance fees. The building reuses rainwater, has 17 homes, wooden construction, a shared laundry and a small garden.

In Germany, the *Baugruppen* promote participatory planning. Among the Berlin *Baugruppen* is the Spreefeld complex (2014) [fig. 106] by Silvia Carpaneto, fatkoehl architekten and BARarchitekten. It has 64 apartments, and two-thirds of the grounds are left free for a series of spaces — open to non-residents as well — including cultural projects and community activities. Likewise, in Amsterdam, the Vrijburcht building (2007) [fig. 107] by CASA Architecten and the Vrijburcht foundation, has 52 dwellings with three different typologies, commercial spaces, common services, a restaurant, a centre for the disabled, a nursery and an orchard. The homes extend outwards through open walkways arranged around a large central courtyard, while a garden generates a microenvironment that is as sheltered as it is open.

Another important place of reference for housing cooperatives based on the model of collective ownership and limited equity is Uruguay. Although housing cooperatives only make up about 3% of the country's housing stock, their impact has been significant: from a series of pilot projects at the end of the 1960s, they went from 95 homes to 10,000 in ten years. Later, between 2005 and 2020, nearly 15,000 homes were built.[19] The FUCVAM (Uruguayan Federation of Housing Cooperatives for Mutual Aid) includes people who cannot save up the required capital, and instead contribute with labour work during the

107

106

construction process. The work of FUCVAM is exemplified in the Nuevo Amanecer Housing Complex (Montevideo, 1971), designed by José Luis Livni. The complex is home to more than 1,500 people, and has a library, collective spaces, a nursery, sports areas and a primary school.

In the United States, housing cooperatives or "co-ops" make up only 1% of the housing stock, but given the scale of the country, this means almost 1.2 million homes. Around half of the American co-ops are located in Manhattan, and are apartment buildings on the open market. However, the need for affordable housing is changing the dynamics, and new cooperative housing projects are springing up in different parts of the country. Co-ops for low-income housing generally exist thanks to community land trusts, which also operate in the United

Kingdom, Belgium and Canada. In Quebec, there are inclusive cooperatives to house migrants, people with disabilities and those who need care. In many cases, housing cooperatives are not simply a solution to the housing crisis, but in fact an adaptable spatial instrument to oppose the structures that cause and perpetuate said crisis. Palo Alto (1972) is the first modern and most important housing cooperative in Mexico City, and the words of one of its 1,400 inhabitants exemplifies the situation: "Without collective property, there is no cooperative. Without it, for us, the urban poor, our only destiny would have been eternal rent, and what I call the *salaries of death*, because you only stop working by dying."[20] A large sign placed on one of the murals in the public spaces of Palo Alto — known as the affordable housing neighbourhood with the most collective services and community spaces in the capital of Mexico — reflects the key contribution of one particular group: "Without women there is no cooperative."

All of these projects are based on a combination of ideas found in the Cooperative Housekeeping movement of the pioneers of domestic science; the logic of the minimum in Hannes Meyer's Co-op Interieur; the comfort of Charlotte Perriand's apartments; the participatory processes promoted by Christopher Alexander; and the convergence of diversity defended by Lucien Kroll. In other words, they bring together freedom, efficiency, wellbeing and identity, which all coexist by changing up domestic conventions and thinking about evolving needs.

As for public housing, the most notable examples are found in Europe, where there is a long tradition of social housing: in Vienna alone, 62% of all inhabitants live in social housing, compared to 5% in New York.[21] Generally, in the United States, the need to access affordable housing is resolved by individuals. In many cases, this happens inside houses made for large families but which are now shared with others: 30% of adults live with at least one other adult, over 24 years of age, with whom he or she has no romantic relationship.[22] Most of the residential

108

land in the United States is still designated for single-family detached houses, and in fact it is illegal to build any other type of house on 75% of the residential land in many cities, including Seattle and Chicago.[23] An exemplary case in the United States that seeks to do something about the lack of affordable housing and community living is the Casa Familiar Community Station (San Diego, 2021) [fig. 108], designed by Teddy Cruz and Fonna Forman in the San Ysidro neighbourhood, near the border area with Tijuana. The complex has temporary dwellings, housing for the elderly, a nursery, a small auditorium, a migrant centre and a healthcare centre. It is made up of five longitudinal volumes, each with a different character, that link two streets and encourage interaction by opening the houses on both sides towards the interior corridors.

In Europe, one outstanding example is the public rental housing initiative carried out by the Balearic Housing Institute (IBAVI) in the Balearic Islands from 2019 to 2023, under the leadership of Cris Ballester and Carles Oliver. They focused their efforts on generating open competitions to create affordable housing, with locally-sourced materials and buildings that minimise emissions according to the following statute: "We do not seek to build, we seek to alleviate the housing emergency through the construction of social housing."[24] IBAVI does not sell square metres, but rather it promotes buildings that reuse rainwater and have passive systems to deal with the extreme climate, in a territory where the population doubles during the summer months. In two years, rent debts rates were reduced by 50% as a result of cutting the monthly energy expenditure. In four years, 1,200 homes were built from stone, compacted earth, ceramic and marine plants (that wash up on the beach), with reed pergolas, terraces, gardens and public spaces. IBAVI's solutions during this period are an open dossier on how to smash the hierarchy of housing; this way, housing buildings can accommodate indistinct uses over time and enable innovative solutions designed by young people who want to be as ecological as their great-grandparents. These solutions were criticised because they look like expensive housing and because stone and mud construction is not an option in other countries. However, such critiques seem to have overlooked the fact that the main contribution of this programme is all about making use of what is locally available: one place might have access to stone or straw, while in another there may be demolition debris or abandoned buildings to repurpose.

Three housing projects in the UK offer a diversity of uses, collective spaces, flexibility and integration with the context and society. The social housing projects built on the outskirts of London by Peter Barber in the late 2010s — McGrath Road Housing in Stratford [fig. 109], Ordnance Road in Enfield and Holmes Road Studios for homeless people in Kentish Town — are a reinterpretation of historical typologies such as Victorian terraced houses and cottages. However, these newer projects are more spacious, with green roofs, rear gardens, central courtyards and terraces that overlook the street.

109

These alternatives come about in reaction to the injustices of the neoliberal city model. They are very different to what is usually built in cities, and which Saskia Sassen describes with the following phrase: "A vast stretch of suburban housing is not a city; it is built-up terrain."[25] The peripheries of cities worldwide are growing progressively, ruled over by the use of cars. Although the examples referred to in this section advocate for the regeneration of underutilised areas and the redefinition of the home on the basis of non-blood ties, we are still building houses in keeping with models that made sense over two centuries ago.

1   See Olsson, Lea and Loerakker, Jan, "Revisioning Amsterdam Bijlmermeer", *Failed Architecture*, 26 April 2013: www.failedarchitecture.com/the-story-behind-the-failure-revisioning-amsterdam.
2   Eisenman, Peter (preface), *IAUS*, no. 12 (*John Hejduk, 7 Houses*), New York, 1980.
3   Lerup, Lars, *Planned Assaults*, Montreal/Cambridge (Mass.): Canadian Centre for Architecture/The MIT Press, 1987.
4   Frank, Suzanne, *Peter Eisenman's House VI. The Client's Response*, New York: Whitney Library of Design, 1994.
5   Ibid., p. 38.
6   Johnson, Philip and Wigley, Mark, *Deconstructivist Architecture* (exhibition catalogue), New York: The Museum of Modern Art, 1988.
7   See Solà-Morales, Ignasi de, "Liquid Architecture", in Davidson, Cynthia C. (ed.), *Anyhow*, New York/Cambridge, (Mass.): Anyone Corporation/The MIT Press, 1998, p. 38.
8   Ito, Toyo, "Una arquitectura que pide un cuerpo androide" [1998], in Torres Nadal, José María (ed.), *Toyo Ito. Escritos*, Murcia: COAAT, 2000, p. 65.
9   See Taki, Koji, "Conversation with Kazuyo Sejima", *El Croquis*, no. 77 (*Kazuyo Sejima 1988-1996*), Madrid, 1996, p. 23.
10 Ishigami, Junya, "On Freedom in Architecture", *El Croquis*, no. 182, (*Junya Ishigami 2005-2015*), Madrid, 2016, p. 230.
11 Zhang, Lily (ed.), *Freeing Architecture. Junya Ishigami*, Tokyo: Fondation Cartier pour l'art contemporain/LIXIL Publishing, 2018, pp. 5-9.
12 See Druot, Frédéric; Lacaton, Anne and Vassal, Jean-Philippe, *Plus: Large Scale Housing Development. An Exceptional Case*, Barcelona: Editorial Gustavo Gili, 2007.
13 Aravena, Alejandro and Iacobelli, Andrés, *Incremental Housing and Participatory Design Manual*, Ostfildern: Hatje Cantz, 2012, p. 37.
14 Heringer, Anna, *Essential Beauty*, Madrid: Fundación ICO/Arquitectura Viva, 2022, p. 206.
15 Ibid., p. 206, Laufen Manifesto for a Humane Design Culture, with Andres Lepik among others.
16 Ibid., p. 106.
17 See Hugentobler, Margrit; Hofer, Andreas and Simmendinger, Pia (eds.), *More Than Housing. Cooperative Planning: A Case Study in Zürich*, Basel: Birkhäuser, 2016.
18 LaCol and La Ciutat Invisible, *Habitar en comunidad. La vivienda cooperativa en cesión de uso*, Madrid: Catarata, 2020, p. 27.
19 Ibid., p. 19.

[20] Santoyo-Orizco, Ivonne, *A Militant Way of Living*, Places Journal, March 2023: https://placesjournal.org/article/cooperativa-palo-alto-housing-mexico-city.

[21] See Day, Meagan, "We Can Have Beautiful Public Housing", *Jacobin Magazine*, 13, November 2018: www.jacobinmag.com.

[22] Paone, Fabrizio and Sampieri, Angelo (eds.), *ReHab. Living, Inhabitants, Houses*, Berlin: Jovis Verlag, 2022, p. 289.

[23] Badger, Emily and Bui, Quoctrung, "Cities Start to Question an American Ideal: A House with a Yard on Every Lot", *The New York Times*, New York, July 19, 2019.

[24] Obal, Liliana, "Protected Public Housing, An Alternative Model, A conversation with Cris Ballester Parets and Carles Oliver Barceló", *El Croquis*, no. 219 (*IBAVI 2019-2023, a collective research*), Madrid, 2023, p. 17.

[25] Saskia Sassen. "¿Does the City Have *Speech*?", in Hernández Gálvez, Alejandro (ed.). *Habla ciudad*, Mexico City: Arquine, 2014, p. 15.

After the House

More Than Houses

"Against the ideology of the domestic which our generation neither can afford, nor desires."

Dogma and Black Square

In the 2020s — a decade marked by the lockdowns of the Covid-19 pandemic, in houses proven to be recurrently insufficient — housing explorations focus on creating alternatives for a non-domestic future. That is, to generate something else between the spaces designated for sleeping and those designated for working or socialising, and creating spaces where resources are not wasted. In the twentieth century, the nuclear attacks on Hiroshima and Nagasaki raised real questions about the future of humankind, which laid in the hands of a few individuals who could destroy cities at the push of a button. Today, however, the concern is more about day-to-day human actions and how they affect the planet. This is of particular interest now, at a time when the minimum parameters of housing are once again being disputed — parameters that were seemingly established more than a hundred years ago with the laws for basic housing in different parts of the world. For example, in many cities rooms are once again being built without windows, without any natural light or ventilation. Given that housing as a human right is still inaccessible to millions, the objective of this era is not only to improve habitability, but to extend it to more people.

The demolition in 2017 of Alison and Peter Smithson's Robin Hood Gardens in London — a complex praised by renowned architects, despised by developers who wanted to build higher density housing on the land, and defended by some inhabitants of the complex but criticised by others — exemplifies the vacuum in which political, urban and social decisions take place regarding housing, faced with the industry's might as a global financial instrument. While the buildings in Robin Hood Gardens were demolished less than fifty years after they were completed, parts of the façade are displayed as relics in art centres. This shows the extreme views about built heritage and the definition of what is desirable in a home. When considering that houses represent 80% of the buildings in cities,[1] it is clear that by improving the house the world is automatically improved too. However, to do so we must think about everything outside of the bed, and remember that the house, far from being a private domain, is a political sphere, and far from being a place of comfort, it has been a space associated with exploitation and isolation.

Two exhibitions held at the MoMA in New York mark the end of one era and the beginning of another in which architecture started to move away from itself to see if it could thus respond to crucial problems: *Fore-Closed: Rehousing the American Dream* (2012) and *Uneven Growth: Tactical Urbanisms for Expanding Megacities* (2014). The first highlighted the devastation of the land caused by the repetition of the single-family "American Dream" home throughout the twentieth century; the second showed the polarisation of societies due to housing inequality, with increasingly devastating effects, especially following the crisis triggered by the 2008 housing market crash which brought the global economy to its knees. Both exhibitions followed up another one, *Rising Currents* (MoMA, 2010), which called for the reinvention of urban infrastructure in light of the effects of climate change, particularly on the New York waterfront, although these changes could well be applied to many cities. All over the world, the consequences of climate catastrophes show the effects of human actions caused by neglecting nature's balance. Therefore, *Foreclosed: Rehousing the American Dream* prompted the following question: if we could change our dreams and aspirations about housing, would we be able to change our cities?

Creating new axioms

Changing our dreams means changing the words that define what we strive for. The terms we use to describe the rooms in a house can be counted just with our fingers: bedroom, kitchen, dining room, living room and bathroom, and little else. Historically, however, there used to be far more varied terminology that reflects other alternatives: for example, the "round rooms" of Mexico, where an entire house would fit inside a multi-purpose space in which a large household group could live, or the medieval Dutch houses with a "front room" for commercial uses and a "back room" for a variety of activities. Sometimes, spaces' names were strict descriptions of their functions, such as the Victorian "drawing room". At other times, the terms have been more evocative, such as the "room of echoes" and the "coincidence room" proposed by Nieuwenhuys. Today we have, at most, the distinction of "wet areas", or "fixed areas". The house might be split into a "day zone" and a "night zone", which contain rooms used exclusively for sleeping and spaces where we receive guests only a few days a year. This lack of alternative room names reflects the slow renewal of the domestic space. Today, we can shop at the supermarket without leaving home, or work anywhere in the world from the sofa in our living room — but how do we incorporate the diversity of uses and users into domestic solutions that have barely changed over the last two centuries?

In the book *Species of Spaces* (1974),[2] Georges Perec imagined the home being arranged by sensory functions ("seeery", "smeelery" and "feelery") or the days of the week ("Mondayery, Tuesdayery, Wednesdayery"). He suggested that there should be a room that serves no purpose, "the useless room", which in fact is useful for everything, or a "room without a name" to host indeterminate actions. The term "room without a name" was popularised in *Tomorrow's House* (1945)[3] by George Nelson and Henry Wright, a book that defined the modern way of living. However, fearing the social and political effects of these non-specific rooms — outside of the State's control, and of potentially ambiguous morality — in 1950 the term was replaced with "the family TV room", which lives on in the present day as the centrepiece of the domestic realm.[4]

The power of the nomenclature of a room can be seen in the influence of Virginia Woolf, who stressed the need for "a room of one's own",[5] for the liberation of those who lacked somewhere they could call their own, within the very space where they spent almost their entire lives. The simple act of putting a bolt on a door signified the ability to be oneself, and all that implied. Many of the terms which almost invariably define our lives today are relatively new. The first reference to the "right to privacy" dates from 1890, and the term "nuclear family" (husband, wife and children) only emerged in the 1940s. This concept of the "nuclear family" gave rise to the single-family house, now the most widespread type of dwelling, despite the fact that today more than half of all houses are only inhabited by one or two people; in Berlin and Munich, for example, less than 20% of the population matches this model.[6] Given the urgency of updating how we live by means of architecture, we need to reclaim our own world by using words that define how we want to live: rooms for more than just watching a screen, or houses that are not only for storing belongings and cars.

Houses are made from roofs, walls, doors, windows and floors, so how can we open up and expand what happens in those few square metres, always made from the same handful of parts? The richness of experiences is missing in language, and also in our spaces. When struggling to define the very English term "cosiness", Adolf Loos described it as "the dog by the fireside".[7] In turn, Michael Pollan uses the term "houseness"[8] to express the deep meaning of shelter or the sense of a home, and he uses "doorness" to describe not only the qualities of a door, but the experiences and everything that a door can evoke.[9] Houses are not only the place where people dream, but they are also the representation of their dreams and expectations. This is why Gaston Bachelard believed it was impossible to write the history of the human subconscious without writing the history of the house.[10] How can we articulate something when there are no words or images to describe it? Only by trying out solutions that are not prescribed will we be able to reach interesting new places, in order to create special spaces in collective housing buildings. That way, housing could become a monument to the civic that connects us with the environment.

Inserting blank pages into more projects — so that everyone can write the script of their own life — involves a redefinition of the house. However, this does not happen by designing abstract cells, all with the same characteristics: rooms that measure 2.8 square metres, which could either become a bedroom, a kitchen, a place to work or a space for children to play in. The concept of the house as a single minimal room, to insert whatever we want, in fact ends up leaving little space for anything. It works well in drawings, with attractive furniture arrangements, but it is far from a free interpretation of space, and does not necessarily enable connection with others and the outside. The collective spirit of housing must go beyond the relabelling of lobbies as public agoras, the small protuberances jutting out of façades being called terraces, or corridors being described as public congregation spaces.

Creating new formats for shared living

"Our" architecture barely contemplates spaces for tired bodies, for bodies that breastfeed, for those who want to play or need a place to cry. The definition of "user" should include those who transport the materials used to create these spaces, or those who collect the rubbish. We need to shine a light on what architecture has been hiding for decades: the relationship with the elements that define our subsistence, such as water (hidden in pipes), waste (out of sight and, therefore, not our responsibility), the relationship with the outside world (denied) and the connection with others (those who come to mind, as well as those who do not). We have become separated from the basic elements for survival. However, each project allows us to consider what we would like to reconnect with.

Are there any alternatives to the two predominant housing models of the last two centuries, i.e. the single-family home and the apartment building? Recent coinages that allude to new options — co-living, co-housing, live-work, superliving communities, studio flats and superlofts — are, in most cases, just ploys of the real estate market. Such terms try to sell a false idea of renewed lifestyles in the form of smaller and smaller rooms, albeit with unlimited Internet access and the chance to share a corridor called the shared kitchen. These kinds of attempts — based on a combination of the advantages of the Airbnb model, the serviced hotel, boarding houses and the hippie communal house — are not new living options, but rather the simple shoving-together of minimal rooms that, together, do not make up cooperative houses nor do they build a common habitat. In most new housing projects of this type, the only things that really get collectivised are noises and smells.

Creating caring homes

Five theoretical proposals, presented at the Venice Biennale of Architecture, point towards new paths. Casa Madre (2008) by Andrea Branzi, a former member of Archizoom, consists of three transparent boxes raised on pilotis inside a large aviary-like structure, with alcoves placed within a habitable wall, as if the houses were shelves in a bookshop. He proposes the cohabitation of people and animals, technology and religion, and life and work. Casa Madre is a synthesis of Branzi's decades-long efforts to create cities without architecture: he has sought to free the human being from the formal structures that enclose and divide, and surmount the boundaries between public and private, artificial and natural, work and leisure. Casa Madre breaks down the house, to domesticate the city by turning it into an expanded home for all.

The *Home Economics* exhibition, held in the Biennale's British pavilion in 2016 — curated by Shumi Bose, Jack Self and Finn Williams — showed a different distribution of belongings, according to five time periods, i.e. hours, days, months, years and decades. The idea was to think about how to increase the possibilities of spaces and experiences, as well as the number of people who have access to a desirable place to live. By understanding the house based on the concept of sharing time, different spaces are composed, without the current limitations of day uses and night uses. It questions what things we are willing to collectivise, from a vacuum cleaner to a pillow. For example, the installation *Months*, created by Dogma (Pier Vittorio Aureli and Martino Tattara) and Black Square (Maria Shéhérezade Giudici), is a shared space where a high totem contains a minimal housing core for short stays, designed to reduce domestic labour. In turn, the installation *Decades*, by members of the Hesselbrand studio, shows a home not divided by rooms, but by areas according to the differing conditions of darkness/light, dry/wet, hard/soft. These proposals imply a criticism of the systems of exploitation embedded within the current housing model, such as, for example, the idea of marriage as a source of free domestic work, the creation of houses that are increasingly connected digitally but ever more isolated from each other, the house as a factory for producing new consumers, and housing being placed in the hands of private owners (whereby bureaucrats are the true architects of houses).

The 2021 Venice Biennale of Architecture revolved around questioning the role of current architecture, in order to bring in what we often leave out: plants, animals, water, air, bacteria, etc. That is, all the voices that ought to be considered if we are to shape a common future. We would speak of homes as a kind of Noah's Ark to include phenomena that are beyond our control; the implication is that human beings are no longer the centre of the world, although we are one of its main custodians, and that Noah's Ark is no longer an isolated vessel, but a place for exchange, an accumulation of flows with no division between inside and outside. The need to postpone the Venice Biennale from 2020 to 2021, due to the global crisis caused by the Covid-19 pandemic, is in itself a reflection of the tough question posed opportunely by its curator Hashim Sarkis in the that biennale's title: *How will we live together?* In the 2021 Biennale, *The Opposite Shore* stands out, a work by Dogma: it seeks to transform underused single-family houses in the suburbs by means of interventions, on various scales, that encourage interaction between people, the exterior and mixed uses.

The exhibition *Home Sweet Home* (2023), held at the Triennale di Milano, featured a different work by Dogma, called *Longhouse*. Again, it encourages reuse, in this case of the linear "longhouse", a building type used in various parts of the world as the quintessential collective dwelling. The aim was to reveal various anthropological ways to live together, where the space of shelter is the same as that of ritualisation, rest, productivity, the development of individuality and cooperativeness. *Home Sweet Home*, curated by Nina Bassoli, celebrates the Triennale's centenary with an exhibition about exhibitions of the domestic space. Bassoli takes the theme of care as a common thread, as a founding act of life and the key aspect on which to base any housing project. *Home Sweet Home* recalls some aspects of the *WomanHouse* (1972) exhibition, created by Judy Chicago and Miriam Shapiro in an abandoned house in Hollywood, featuring a series of installations and performances by female artists who transformed the house over the course of a month to exhibit the most destructive aspects of the domestic sphere. Fifty years after the legendary *WomanHouse* exhibition, we still seem more concerned about taking care of our houses than ensuring that our houses take care of us. Fostering caring cities means starting at home: homes must be more than just houses, and more people should have access to good homes.

Creating not just rooms but communities

If we were to imagine housing projects that synthesise the five ideals discussed over the course of this book, we would come up with houses that make us free, that don't waste our time and resources, that provide us with wellbeing, help us be who we want to be and allow us to coexist with others and with the world. Since more has been built in the last 75 years than during the previous seven millennia, the relationship between architecture, actions and territory will become increasingly critical.[11] Some say that it is not necessary to continue building, and we should only refurbish the underused spaces that we already have. Others say that in the next fifteen years, a billion new homes will have to be built.[12] In any case, it is estimated that, in a couple of years, 30% of city dwellers will be living in slums.[13] Cities will exacerbate the contradictions between minimal needs and insatiable desires, between subsistence and wastefulness, and between the advantages of sharing and the refusal to cooperate.

Buildings are the largest economic asset in the world: they make up three times the global gross domestic product.[14] However, the planet's most powerful financial pillar cannot continue to be one of the most destructive. This means rethinking the notions of privacy and coexistence, as well as those of production, consumption and rest, in a world that we have invented for ourselves but which is now beyond our control. Above all, the challenge is learning how to build without damaging. Let us not forget that recurring housing models are not the best ones, but rather the most profitable for investors and politicians. Thus, changing architecture implies transforming laws and the very notion of shelter.

If we want to bridge the gap between houses and what we desire of them, we need to regard the home as something that does not reproduce divisions of class, gender, age and activities. Defining a place of one's own does imply demarcating it in some way, so our future will depend on how we establish these demarcations. Therefore, the mechanisms of individual land ownership must be reconsidered, so that the desire for privacy is compatible with the needs of others and with the careful use of resources. The house is a base, a starting point from which we can address the vast discrepancies between some people's desires and everybody else's needs. If just one thing can be learned from the architects discussed in this book, it is that if we want to change the world, we must start by transforming the house.

Julio Cortázar's short story *House Taken Over* (1951) is more enlightening than hundreds of specialised publications on residential architecture. Cortázar tells the story of Iris and her brother, who share the house in which their ancestors had lived. Suddenly, they feel that their home has been invaded, taken over, by someone or something. They decide to move to the other half of the house, cut off from their belongings, from what defines their life. But then this part of the house starts to seem alien to them as well, to the point that, one day, they finally flee the house in terror, with nothing but what they were wearing, expelled from a home that no longer belongs to them. The story ends when Iris and her brother leave what was once their home, their life, and throw the house key down a drain, lest someone else should think of entering the house that had been taken over. Cortázar speaks of the sense of deterritorialisation within the home, of houses that do not feel like one's own, of detachment and the loss of the home. Where are we heading with all these useless houses, with houses and cities that don't feel like our own? Let's invent all the ways of living that the twenty-first century needs!

1   Montaner, Josep Maria; Muxi, Zaida and Falagán, David H., *Herramientas para habitar el presente, La vivienda del siglo XXI*, Barcelona: Universitat Politècnica de Catalunya, 2011, p. 37.

2   Perec, Georges, *Species of Spaces and Other Pieces*, London: Penguin Books, 1997.

3   Nelson, George and Wright, Henry, *Tomorrow's House*, New York: Simon & Schuster, 1945.

4   See Heller, Dana, *Family Plots: The De-Oedipalization of Popular Culture*, Philadelphia: University of Pennsylvania Press, 1995.

5   See Woolf, Virginia, *A Room of One's Own*, London: The Hogarth Press, 1929.

6   See Maak, Niklas, *Wohnkomplex: warum wir andere Häuser brauchen*, Munich: Carl Hanser Verlag, 2014, p. 14.

7   See Bosma, Koos; Van Hoogstraten, Dorine and Vos, Martijn (eds.), *Housing for the Millions, John Habraken and the SAR (1960-2000)*, Rotterdam: NAi, 2000, p. 31.

8   See Pollan, Michael, *A Place of My Own: The Education of an Amateur Builder*, London: Bloomsbury, 1997, p. 16.

9   Ibid., p. 72.

10 Bachelard, Gaston, *The Poetics of Space*, New York: Orion Press, 1964.

11 See Ingersoll, Richard, "Reduce, Reuse, Recycle", *Arquitectura Viva*, no. 220, Madrid, December 2019, p. 80.

12 See Maak, Niklas, *op. cit.*, p. 17.

13 Ibid., p. 204.

14 De Graaf, Reiner, *architect, verb: The New Language of Building*, New York/London: Verso, 2023, p. 1.

Acknowledgments

To my parents and my grandmother, who gave me a home and taught me what's outside.

To my sisters, who are my home wherever I go.

To Carlos, and to my children María and Francisco, who constantly show me different purposes of homemaking.

To the books that have introduced me to the infinite worlds related to the house.

To my clients who have given me the opportunity to design different ways of living.

To Moisés Puente, who has made this publication possible, and to the Centro para el Futuro de las Ciudades at the Tecnológico de Monterrey for their ongoing support.

Image sources

All images are the author's except: 12: from *E 1027: maison en bord de mer*, Marseilles: Éditions Imbernon, 2015; 13, 14, 18 and 34: from Boesiger, Billy (ed.), *Le Corbusier et Pierre Jeanneret: Oeuvre complète 1910-1929*, Basel: Birkhäuser, 1995; 19: from Hilberseimer, Ludwig, *La arquitectura de la gran ciudad*, Barcelona: Editorial Gustavo Gili, 1999; 21 and 24: from Bergdoll, Barry et al., *Frank Lloyd Wright: Unpacking the Archive,* New York: Museum of Modern Art, 2017; 25: from Marks, Robert and Fuller, R. Buckminster, *Richard Buckminster. The Dymaxion World of Buckminster Fuller*, New York: Anchor Press/Doubleday, 1973; 26: from Riley, Terence and Bergdoll, Barry, *Mies in Berlin*, New York: The Museum of Modern Art, 2001; 28: from *Frederick Kiesler 1890-1965. En el interior de la Endless House* (exhibition catalogue), Valencia: IVAM, 1997; 29: from Van den Heuvel, Dirk and Risselada, Max (eds.), *Alison y Peter Smithson: de la casa del futuro a la casa de hoy*, Barcelona: Polígrafa, 2007; 31: from Banham, Reyner, "A Home Is Not a House", *Art in America,* 1965; 33 and 35: from Lapuerta, Jose María de, *AV Monografías (Casas de maestros)*, Madrid, 2008; 36: from Lichtenstein, Claude and Krausse, Joachim, *Your Private Sky: Discourse, R. Buckminster Fuller*, Baden: Lars Müller, 2001; 39: photograph by Esther McCoy, from Arellano, Iván, *Casa O'Gorman: habitando la cueva (1949-1969)*, PhD, Universitat Politècnica de Catalunya, Barcelona, 2016; 40 and 41: from Friedman, Alice T., *Women and the Making of the Modern House*, New York: Harry N. Abrams, 2006; 43: from Drexler, Arthur, *Ludwig Mies van der Rohe*, New York: George Braziller, 1960; 44: from Bonduki, Nabil (ed.), *Affonso Eduardo Reidy*, Rio de Janeiro: Blau, 2000; 47: from Wigley, Mark, *Constant's New Babylon*, Rotterdam: Witte de With Center for Contemporary Art/010 Publishers, 1998; 48: from Orazi, Manuel et al., *Yona Friedman: The Dilution of Architecture*, Zurich:

Park Books, 2015; 49: from Spiller, Neil, *Visionary Architecture: Blueprints of the Modern Imagination,* New York: Thames & Hudson, 2007; 50 and 51: from Mastrigli, Gabriele, *Superstudio, opere, 1966-1978,* Macerata: Quodlibet, 2016; 52: from Quesada, Fernando (ed.), *Comunidad, común, comuna,* Madrid: Ediciones Asimétricas, 2015; 53: from *Kisho Kurokawa. Metabolism and Symbiosis,* Berlin: Jovis, 2005; 54: from Bosma, Koos et al., *Housing for the Millions, John Habraken and the SAR (1960- 2000),* Rotterdam: NAi Publishers, 2000; 56 and 72: from Bergdoll, Barry and Christensen, Peter, *Home Delivery: Fabricating the Modern Dwelling* (exhibition catalogue), New York: The Museum of Modern Art, 2008; 61: from French, Hilary, *Vivienda colectiva paradigmática del siglo xx,* Barcelona: Editorial Gustavo Gili, Barcelona, 2009; 65: from Dos Santos, José Paulo et al., *Álvaro Siza: obras y proyectos 1954-1992,* Barcelona: Editorial Gustavo Gili, 1996; 75: Peter Eisenman; 77 and 78: Toyo Ito; 79; from *El Croquis,* no. 99 (*Kazuyo Sejima Ryue Nishizawa: 1995-2000*), Madrid, 2001; 80: SANAA; 81 and 82: Junya Ishigami; 94 and 95: from Montaner, Josep Maria, *Después del movimiento* moderno, Barcelona: Editorial Gustavo Gili, 1993; and 98: Yuri Naruse and Jun Inokuma.